Theology After Deleuze

Deleuze Encounters

Series Editor: Ian Buchanan, Professor of Critical and Cultural Theory, University of Wollongong, Australia

The *Deleuze Encounters* series provides students in philosophy and related subjects with concise and accessible introductions to the application of Deleuze's work in key areas of study. Each book demonstrates how Deleuze's ideas and concepts can enhance present work in a particular field.

Series titles include:

Cinema After Deleuze
Richard Rushton

Philosophy After Deleuze
Joe Hughes

Political Theory After Deleuze
Nathan Widder

Space and Place After Deleuze
Arun Saldanha

Theology After Deleuze

KRISTIEN JUSTAERT

Deleuze Encounters

continuum

Continuum International Publishing Group
The Tower Building   80 Maiden Lane
11 York Road   Suite 704
London   New York
SE1 7NX   NY 10038

www.continuumbooks.com

© Kristien Justaert 2012

All rights reserved. No part of this publication may be reproduced or transmitted in any form or by any means, electronic or mechanical, including photocopying, recording, or any information storage or retrieval system, without prior permission in writing from the publishers.

Author has asserted his/her right under the Copyright, Designs and Patents Act, 1988, to be identified as Author of this work.

British Library Cataloguing-in-Publication Data
A catalogue record for this book is available from the British Library.

ISBN: HB: 978-1-4411-9183-0
PB: 978-1-4411-5890-1

Library of Congress Cataloging-in-Publication Data
Justaert, Kristien.
Theology after Deleuze/Kristien Justaert.
pages cm. – (Deleuze encounters)
Includes bibliographical references and index.
ISBN 978-1-4411-5890-1 (pbk. : alk. paper) –
ISBN 978-1-4411-9183-0 (hardcover : alk. paper) –
ISBN 978-1-4411-0217-1 (ebook epub : alk. paper) –
ISBN 978-1-4411-3736-4 (ebook pdf : alk. paper)
1. Deleuze, Gilles, 1925–95.
2. Political theology.
3. Feminist theology. I. Title.
B2430.D454J87 2012
230–dc23
2011047330

Typeset by Deanta Global Publishing Services, Chennai, India

Contents

Acknowledgements vi
Abbreviations vii

Introduction: On life 1

1 Immanent life 11

  Immanent Deleuze 12
  The problem of immanence in theology and the future of immanent theologies 32

2 Spiritual life 39

  Spiritual Deleuze 41
  Becoming-divine with Meister Eckhart and the Chinese 59

3 Creative life 71

  Creative Deleuze 72
  Theologies of creation – creative theologies 86

4 Ethical life 101

  Political Deleuze 104
  Liberation theologies 119

Conclusion: The 'evangelical power' of Deleuze – towards a theology of life 131

Notes 135
Bibliography 149
Index 155

Acknowledgements

I'm extremely grateful to my colleague and friend Colby Dickinson who was so kind to read the complete manuscript of this book. His corrections, comments and support were absolutely indispensable. Also Trevor Maine's contributions to the text were enriching and incredibly helpful. Without the encouragement and support from Ian Buchanan, I would have never had the chance to even write this book – my debt to him is invaluable. I am grateful to the people at Continuum who did a wonderful job in following up on the progress of the manuscript and editing it afterwards. My collaboration with Jacques Haers at the Centre for Liberation Theologies has provided a permanent and fertile breeding ground for many ideas that emerge in this book and I am very grateful for all the chances that he gives me. A grant from the Research Foundation in Flanders, Belgium (FWO-Vlaanderen) has made the writing of this book possible. Finally, thank you Tom and Juno for creating a wonderful home and way of living together.

Abbreviations

To increase the readability of this book, I have chosen to cite the works of Deleuze (and Guattari) in their English translations where possible. Where it was necessary to clarify the meaning of a particular word or phrase, I have also mentioned the French term(s).

AO	Deleuze, G. and Guattari, F. (2004), *Anti-Oedipus. Capitalism and Schizophrenia* (trans. R. Hurley, M Seem, H. R. Lane). London: Continuum.
ATP	Deleuze, G. and Guattari, F. (2004), *A Thousand Plateaus. Capitalism and Schizophrenia* (trans. B. Massumi). London: Continuum.
B	Deleuze, G. (1991), *Bergsonism* (trans. H. Tomlinson & B. Habberjam). New York: Zone Books.
C2	Deleuze, G. (1989), *Cinema 2. The Time-Image* (trans. H. Tomlinson & R. Galeta). London: The Athlone Press.
D	Deleuze, G. and Parnet, C. (2006), *Dialogues II* (trans. H. Tomlinson & B. Habberjam). London: Continuum.
DI	Deleuze, G. (2004), *Desert Islands and Other Texts 1953–74* (trans. M. Taormina). Los Angeles: Semiotext(e).
DR	Deleuze, G. (2004), *Difference and Repetition* (trans. P. Patton). London: Continuum.
EP	Deleuze, G. (1992), *Expressionism in Philosophy: Spinoza* (trans. M. Joughin). New York: Zone Books.
F	Deleuze, G. (2006), *The Fold* (trans. T. Conley). London: Continuum.
K	Deleuze, G. and Guattari, F. (1986), *Kafka. Toward a Minor Literature* (trans. D. Polan). Minneapolis: University of Minnesota Press.

ABBREVIATIONS

LS   Deleuze, G. (1990), *The Logic of Sense* (trans. M. Lester). New York: Columbia University Press.

N   Deleuze, G. (1995), *Negotiations 1972–90* (trans. M. Joughin). New York: Columbia University Press.

NP   Deleuze, G. (2006), *Nietzsche and Philosophy* (trans. H. Tomlinson). New York: Columbia University Press.

PP   Deleuze, G. (1988), *Spinoza: Practical Philosophy* (trans. R. Hurley). San Francisco: City Light Books.

TRM   Deleuze, G. (2007), *Two Regimes of Madness. Texts and Interviews 1975–95* (trans. A. Hodges & M. Taormina). Los Angeles: Semiotext(e).

WP   Deleuze, G. and Guattari, F. (1994), *What is Philosophy?* (trans. H. Tomlinson & G. Burchell). New York: Columbia University Press.

Introduction: On life

I am the way, the truth and the life (John 14:6).

A free man thinks of nothing less than of death, and his wisdom is a meditation, not on death, but on life (Spinoza, Ethics IV, 67).

Life. A simple, one-word summary of what constitutes, in my opinion, the most important key to the connection between Deleuze and theology. Deleuze and theology, it could be said, share a passion for life, for a specific kind of life even. The importance of 'life' as a theological and religious category can hardly be overestimated: no matter how we define who or what God or the divine is, what counts in the end is to what extent believers succeed in *attuning* their lives to the divine life, in fact *by living a divine life*. Christian theologians, for example, interpret the life of Jesus Christ as the ultimate expression of *who God is*; they call for an *Imitatio Christi* as an authentic following of Christ ('discipleship'). The divine life is the eternal life, and Christ's resurrection three days after his death reveals how a divine life always surmounts death. In Deleuze's works too, the concept of life becomes a key term for any interpretation of his philosophy that wishes to offer an encompassing view of his thought. This fact can be glimpsed by the manner in which his metaphysics is inspired by Spinoza, whom he reads as a practical philosopher, as well as by a vitalist like Bergson and someone like Nietzsche who actually *lived* his philosophy. Moreover, it seems as if Deleuze considers his own thinking as practical (or political or ethical), even *before* it could be considered as metaphysical: 'politics comes before being' (ATP, 203).

In Deleuze's writings, I distinguish four central characteristics of Life (as he conceives of it) that can lead to a 'rereading' of (certain aspects of) theology. These characteristics will constitute the skeleton of this book. In the following paragraph, I will only sketch their contours and will subsequently elaborate on them further in the rest of the book.

Life is an immanent process for Deleuze (Chapter 1). It takes place on a 'plane' of immanence, which can be described as a transcendental field. The conditions for life, in other words, are immanent to that life. There exists no hierarchy on this plane (all beings and events are equal expressions of being), for hierarchy would reintroduce the transcendence of one thing to another. It is also a life of spirituality, for it is no small task for human beings to leave behind their subjectivity (even if this subjectivity is constructed and not given) and be absorbed in the stream of being – to live an impersonal life (Chapter 2). Indeed, for Deleuze, life is primarily the life of being. Living is not something that solely belongs to subjects or human beings. It stretches out to inorganic beings too. In Deleuze's philosophy, there is an emphasis on living over thinking in order to compensate for the traditional privilege of thought over being (indeed, for Deleuze, being *equals* thought), a focus that he extends to life beyond human beings.

Life is also creation and creativity (Chapter 3). The creative aspect of life not only reveals the dynamic core of a life but also stresses the significance of newness generated through endless processes of 'becoming'. And, last but not least, life is a practical matter; it is connected to an 'ethics of life' (Chapter 4). The ethical-political aspect of life is of such paramount importance to Deleuze that I believe he considers this to be the core focus of his philosophy.

Since the main topic of this book is the question of how theology can 'recover' from an encounter with Deleuze (indeed, this meeting can be mind-blowing and even 'revolutionary' for certain theologians), each chapter begins with one of these aforementioned themes in Deleuze's work, each being met with a theological answer that will be formulated in the second part of the chapter. Since no real encounter between Deleuze and theology has been established in the past, these answers are a kind of 'theological experiment': they can take the form of a development in theology, a return to a certain history of theology or the radicalization of an already existing line in theology that has Deleuzian affinities. For the sake of clarity, I will keep the Deleuze part separate from the theological part in each chapter, although it goes without saying that several hints and connections will be made between the 'two parties' throughout the text. Concerning the use of the word 'theology', a certain ambiguity is, I believe, inevitable. First of all, although the encounter between Deleuze and theology should not limit itself to it, I most often refer to *Christian* theology. Within Christian theology, I distinguish (although in practice, the distinction is not always that clear) between what I call the 'visible' and the 'invisible' parts of the tradition. Visible theology would be 'mainstream' theology, or classical theology, or in the case of Catholicism: the theology expressed by the Vatican. It is a collection of doctrines and liturgies based on centuries-old discussions about the meaning of the life, death and resurrection of Jesus Christ. The invisible tradition does not rely less on the life of Jesus but could be considered as a somewhat more radical interpretation of it. It is the tradition of mystical theology and of liberation theologies: a 'tradition' that was always rather marginal and that was looked at rather suspiciously by mainstream believers. For me, the encounter of Deleuze and theology urges theology to rediscover its invisible traditions and to articulate a contemporary theology in line with those.

It is not an easy match, though, Deleuze and theology. Concerning the notion of life, my 'joint-notion' as it were, there is already a certain degree of disagreement present in their relation.

In Christian theology, there is a kind of duality in the understanding of life: on the one hand, life is considered to be a *gift* (from God to beings), and on the other hand, all creatures are called to live a 'divine life' (from beings to God). Which side the pendulum leans towards, that is, which direction is emphasized, depends precisely on how one sees the relationship between the Creator (Life) and the creatures (the living). It is already clear that Deleuze's philosophy will share the most affinities with the second option – with 'life' here being defined as the divine life in which beings can participate – whereas the first option leads to theories of analogy and the safeguarding of God's transcendence (we and our talk about God *depend* on God, though God is independent of us, and so we cannot know whether our God-talk, formulated in human terms, really applies to God).

In line with both Aristotle and Thomas Aquinas, the theory of an analogy of being (*analogia entis*) and the transcendence of God were part of the leading theologies for ages. They still constitute, in fact, the core of classical Christian theology, both catholic and protestant. Living a divine life or finding unity with God was something for the mystics, the happy few who were at once respected within Christianity but also often found themselves on the edges of heresy and excommunication from the church. The marriage between Deleuze and theology will therefore appear in this light as being somewhat forced, and certainly uncommon. The biggest problems from the side of theology would definitely be the lack of *transcendence* in Deleuze's system of thought and as a consequence, the apparent impossibility of making room for something like a divine *revelation*. Indeed, the very condition for the possibility of theology seems to be the recognition of something or someone outside of us – outside of our world – a transcendent entity or person that provides our lives with meaning and that functions as a moral ground. How else could we make room for what goes beyond our capacity for understanding, for that which we cannot speak about, for the transcendent? I will come back to these problems in the next pages.

Deleuze is also an unwilling partner at first sight. If he mentions theology explicitly – which he rarely does – it is mostly in a negative sense.[1] In the eyes of Deleuze, the theological enterprise (which, for Deleuze, corresponds with what I have called the visible theological tradition) keeps the logic of representation alive, and by doing so, it supports the structures of transcendence. Indeed, the logic of representation works with dualisms (the founding one being the dualism between thinking and being); dualisms create hierarchies and hierarchies constitute a space for transcendence to be posited: not all beings are equal. This is a fundamental problem for Deleuze, who believes that Being expresses itself in all beings in the same manner, or, all beings express Being in the same way (although beings differ among themselves).

How can we overcome these objections from both sides of the 'dialogue' or at least circumvent them temporarily so that we might find openings for a fruitful encounter beyond these apparent and obvious obstacles? In what follows, I will try to create openings in both parties, tracking down the 'theological' aspects in Deleuze's thinking and the 'Deleuzian' aspects present within theology. This double approach should allow me to draw some conclusions especially on the side of theology, although we are often left to speculate as to what a theology after Deleuze looks like. I will in the end, however, argue that such a theology would have a strong spiritual as well as a political basis (see Chapter 4).

What kind of openings am I talking about?

The presupposition that constitutes the very basis for this book is that Deleuze's philosophy contains some highly important theological implications. More concretely, I believe, and I wish to defend and demonstrate in this book, that in the literal sense of the word, Deleuze's philosophy is a kind of theo-logy, in the sense that he talks about the Absolute (for Deleuze, that would be Being) and that there is a message of 'salvation' in his thinking, a plea for living a 'real Life', for leaving behind the world of representation, for a life on the plane of immanence. Moreover, the centrality of creativity and the articulation of the relation between Creation/the Creator (in Deleuzian: Being, Life) and the creatures (beings, the living) – articulated as a univocal relation by Deleuze, as opposed to a relation of analogy between God and creatures – point towards a certain 'theological' structure of his system of thought (that he shares with all great metaphysics, especially the premodern systems). Finally, Deleuze's emphasis on the overcoming of the subject and on a new kind of 'community' that contains a political project (though he would rather use the word 'assemblage') can be recognized as features that also belong to most theologies. No doubt, a lot of theologians and philosophers would object to this thesis of a 'theological Deleuze', and they perhaps have good reason to do so, the most important reason being the non-teleological character of Deleuze's metaphysics, as will also become clear in this book. For now, I intend to utilize the affinities present between Deleuze and theology to create openings for a rather productive encounter.

The philosopher who helps us most to discern the theological structures in Deleuze's work, is Spinoza. Throughout this book, Spinoza will implicitly play a key role: on all those aspects of life that we highlight (immanence, spirituality, creativity and ethics), Spinoza influenced Deleuze a great deal. Of course, the emphasis on the Spinozist character of Deleuze's metaphysics is partly motivated by our 'agenda': Nietzsche, Leibniz, Hume and Bergson (among many others) have also left their marks on Deleuze's thinking – though, in our journey to more theological fields, Spinoza is the best guide. After all, it should come as no surprise that Deleuze called Spinoza 'the Christ among all philosophers', the one to whom the other great philosophers are merely apostles that can only approach or move away from this mystery (WP, 60). There are indeed several aspects in Spinoza's philosophy that make him an interesting 'theologian' or that could at least reveal another way of doing theology than the classical theologies of transcendence. Most importantly, Spinoza shows us how one can think about the Absolute (God) in an immanent way. Deleuze adapts this metaphysics, which could bring forth and strengthen a transformation in theology that is yet in a way already partly taking place (see Chapter 1). Second, the shift from morality to ethics (the former belonging to a logic of representation and transcendence), a turn that again marks a devaluation of transcendence, opens up new possibilities for more immanent theologies to counter the common critique that without a transcendent God, there can be no 'ethics'. Third, Spinoza's model of the body (which Deleuze embraces with his concepts of the 'assemblage' or the 'machine') and his parallelism of mind and body, when injected into theology, could have far-reaching consequences for the image of God as well as for the interpretation of relation between God and creation. Before dismissing Spinoza's philosophy (and Deleuze's, for that matter) as 'atheism' or 'pantheism' (two very common reproaches directed towards Spinoza), I want to consider these aspects at length in the following chapters, investigating their possible contributions to theology beyond premature categorizations and judgements.

Every chapter of this book will therefore in a certain sense demonstrate the centrality of Spinoza's ideas within the discussion. And every chapter will in a way stress the importance of politics in the broad sense, that is, of ethics. This movement will culminate in the fourth chapter. In this fashion, not only some core aspects of Spinoza's philosophy but also the main keys of interpretation Deleuze uses in his reading of Spinoza are reflected back to us: the first two chapters testify to Deleuze's reading of Spinoza as a *systematic* philosopher who thinks from God towards beings. Chapter 4 is an expression of a more methodological, *ethical* and political interpretation of Spinoza, a centripetal one that works from beings towards God.[2] These two aspects (systematic and ethical) can also be found in Deleuze's own philosophy, and both can fruitfully result in a conception of a theology that is not a 'classical' theology but one that can defend itself as an immanent theology of life, exceeding the distinction between 'orthodox' and 'heterodox', between visible and invisible, between philosophy and theology. Chapter 3 can therefore be considered as a hinge between the two parts, because it is precisely the creativity of being that allows us to make the transition from the ontological-speculative (Chapters 1 and 2) to the ethical-practical (Chapter 4).

From the side of the visible tradition of theology, I have already mentioned the two most important stumbling blocks for an openness towards Deleuze's legacy: his apparent rejection of transcendence and the impossibility to have an account of revelation. It would seem that without transcendence, there is no critical moment present any longer in one's worldview, no clear distinction between the finite and the infinite, no basis for morality and (moral) judgement. In the first chapter, I will thoroughly comment on the aspect of transcendence in relation to the thought of Deleuze; however, let me already say here that certain forms of transcendence can be discerned in Deleuze's philosophy, although the primacy of immanence is unquestionable. However, an 'immanentization' of theology should not necessarily be a bad thing; it could even be the case that the only way to save God from the trapping logic of representation is to recognize the immanent being of God (see Chapter 1). The move beyond the logic of representation will likewise still allow us to perceive a certain type of revelation. Of course, I am not talking about specific revelations of God that belong to religious traditions. However, in my opinion, the two core aspects of revelation – communication and relation – can also be found in Deleuze's metaphysics. This means that the dimension that lies beyond representation communicates with us in one way or another, it appeals to us, it speaks – and through this appeal, it builds a kind of relation with individuals, or more generally, with the world, with beings. Concerning communication ('what is this dimension actually telling us?'), I will discuss the four themes mentioned above: immanence, spirituality, creativity and ethics. As for the relational component of revelation: it will become clear in the first chapter that the revelation of being connects all beings with their 'source' again, without giving up the differences between these beings. In the third chapter on creativity, then, the notion of relation will play a prominent role.

Moreover, it can be said that today, there is a sort of crisis of transcendence within theology. Not only have certain developments in postmodern thought and positive science questioned the 'transcendent paradigm', more and more theologians have begun to see great value in the concept of immanence and use it to oppose the abuses of power (on the part of theologians or believers) that reinforce the structures of transcendence within religion. Liberation theologies, feminist theologies, postcolonial, contextual and ecotheologies were, from their emergence, interested in a more immanent worldview. Deleuze could encourage those theologies, I would add, to think this immanence even more radically and thoroughly.

Not all theologians will be happy with Deleuze's mixing of the finite and the infinite, with his potential for their profession/passion. An important fear, formulated by John Milbank, is that 'without an openness to transcendent critique, the secular [i.e. the immanent for Milbank] will tend to idolize its own critical impulse and become blind to its own presumptions and limitations'.[3] In spite of these critiques, I want to demonstrate that Deleuze's thought could be a great help for the construction of a theology of the future that honours, celebrates and respects the divine life maybe more than the classical theologies of transcendence. Indeed, through his concepts of life, immanence, creativity and ethics, Deleuze could even help theology to liberate *Godself* from the category of transcendence . . . . This theology will be an immanent one, with a strong spiritual and political programme that constitutes a permanent form of (immanent) critique and that continuously questions and transgresses its own limitations.

I interpret Deleuze's philosophy as a *non-neutral* enterprise, supporting the interpretation that his thinking is not deprived of certain beliefs and of a certain kind of spirituality. We are dealing with a 'great' holistic metaphysics that has premodern aspirations in trying to overcome all dualisms and dichotomies (even the one between beings and God) and creating a solid yet dynamic metaphysics, although one with many postmodern allures, such as the refusal of teleology and the dismissal of hierarchies. This interpretation of Deleuze evidently presupposes a specific relation between philosophy and theology: philosophical 'reason' (ratio, rationality) is not just an instrument used by theology to articulate its own agenda. Philosophy is not subordinate to theology; they both contemplate and question the same reality, each using its specific language. It fits Deleuze's rather premodern conception of metaphysics as an enterprise that encompasses and engages with the whole of reality, with all of its multifaceted domains. Of all the different ways of expressing reality, theology probably stands the closest to philosophy (closer than mathematics or art, for example), because theology and philosophy (could) share the same method and both use intellectual language to say something about the complexity, the functioning and the meaning of reality, although the concepts they use often differ. Theology and (continental) metaphysics also bring reality back to one 'absolute' principle. In theology, this principle is called God; in metaphysics, it can have different names – for Deleuze, it is 'being' or 'life'. But it is not only Deleuze who supports this articulation of the relation between philosophy and theology – the blurring of the boundaries between both disciplines is part of our *Zeitgeist*. In this postsecularist environment, there is no absolute criterion by which to claim that something is theology or philosophy.[4]

However, even if one does not support the intermingling of theology and philosophy and wants to keep the two disciplines separate, it is still possible from the content of this book to consider Deleuze's philosophy as a *mediation* that can at least help theology to see certain aspects of human nature and/or society more clearly, and maybe even help theology to reconnect with its invisible traditions.

Before we embark on this theo-philosophical adventure, let me finish this introduction by saying that Deleuze is a difficult author. I thus propose to read his books like one reads poetry – with a certain openness, intuitively, tentatively, over and over again. The reading should be no less sharp due to what I am calling a poetic reading, however. It is just such a reading that in fact allows diverse and multi-layered resonances to surface within his work.

I will make several connections with Deleuze's thought, though inevitably, a lot of other possible connections are lost. I read Deleuze in a 'practical' way, so to speak. As a consequence, this book will not be a scholarly exegesis of Deleuze's work. The questions that interest me are rather: what are the *effects* of Deleuze's work, what is at stake here in them, how can a theologian who encounters

Deleuze recognize Deleuze's strength and intensity in his thinking about the Absolute for the development of an immanent theology of life? Moreover, the scope of this book does not allow for a thorough reading of all of Deleuze's books. I thus necessarily skip lengthy elaborations on his books on art, the ones on Kafka and Bacon as well as the ones on cinema. They are beautiful 'applications' of his metaphysics, but considering the focus on theology within this book, they are less suitable to the discussion at hand. When Deleuze spoke about his reading of Spinoza at the beginning of his book *Spinoza: Practical Philosophy*, he used the words of Malamud, words that could not be more well chosen:

> I didn't understand every word but when you are dealing with such ideas you feel as though you were taking a witch's ride. After that I wasn't the same [wo]man. . . . (PP, 1)

1

Immanent life

God is really among you! (1 Cor 14:25)

The most important intellectual shock that Deleuze provides to theology is the idea that immanence and not transcendence will bring us 'salvation', or Life. What, in God's name, could this mean? This chapter is meant to lay bare the central place of immanence in Deleuze's philosophy: the so-called 'plane of immanence' is the condition of possibility for doing philosophy in the Deleuzian sense, that is, for creating concepts.

> It is a plane of immanence that constitutes the absolute ground of philosophy, its earth or deterritorialization, the foundation on which it creates its concepts. (WP, 41)

Immanence can indeed be considered as the key term of Deleuze's philosophy, as the 'thread which runs through Deleuze's work as a whole',[1] as Miguel De Beistegui notes – next to 'difference' probably. Both terms, immanence and difference, are synonyms of being, and both terms need to be thought of independently – not in relation, respectively, to 'transcendence' or 'identity' (as will become clear in what follows). In the first part of this chapter, I will try to unveil the meaning of immanence for Deleuze while bearing in mind the main question of this chapter, namely how the idea of immanence could be useful or important for theology too. Indeed, the analysis offered here will focus on immanence in terms of its relation to the Absolute. Deleuze is not the first to connect immanence and the Absolute; there is even a (marginal) theo-philosophical tradition formulated along these lines of thought. That is why I will connect the meaning of immanence in Deleuze with its meaning in the thought of Thomas Aquinas and Duns Scotus (the latter being an important source of inspiration for Deleuze). But despite this theological backdrop, Spinoza definitely remains the one figure who aids Deleuze in formulating his idea of the 'plane of immanence' in the most radical way. Accordingly, in the second part, I will draw a rough scheme of what an immanent theology might look like, referring to a marginal though non-negligible 'tradition' of immanent theologies, both in the past and in the present, as well as try to demonstrate that thinking about God from an immanent perspective might offer contemporary theology a breath of air and possibilities to cope with fundamental theological problems like our God-talk and the general relationship of creatures with God.

Immanent Deleuze

Immanence, transcendence, representation

There are few philosophers who have defended the idea of immanence as explicitly and passionately as Gilles Deleuze. In fact, Deleuze considered immanence not simply as an idea or a concept, but as the *pre-philosophical horizon* against which thinking can be creative and productive. The pre-philosophical character of this horizon, also expressively called the 'plane of immanence' (WP, 35ff), connects philosophy in its very essence with non-philosophers (WP, 43). According to Deleuze, the question of thinking against a transcendent or an immanent horizon is something that concerns philosophers and non-philosophers alike: it defines two totally different world views, two wholly different ways of 'being in the world', and for Deleuze, there is only one world in which life is worth living. In other words, immanence is not (only) a technical philosophical concept, it is a matter of how one lives his or her life.

As such, Deleuze rejects any form of transcendence, connecting it rather with the poisonous 'logic of representation' (DR, 164), the logic we explained in the introduction as a way of thinking in which thought and language represent being(s). What does the logic of representation have to do with transcendence? Representational thinking is synonymous with a world view that can be analyzed as dualistic: on the one hand, there is the human mind (rational thinking), and on the other hand, there is being or beings. Between those two, there is a gap (although, of course, the human mind also 'is', and in this way, is a being in itself). As a consequence, thinking can only *represent* being – it does not and cannot be equal to being, and it never fully coincides with the beings that are its objects.

The dichotomy between thinking and being that is the core of the logic of representation immediately installs a hierarchy between the two poles: thinking wishes to control and rule over being in order to understand it. This reality is why representational thinking can be characterized as a movement towards identification: every being has to be labelled and categorized within existing hierarchies. On the other hand, being transcends thinking in the sense that rationality can never fully grasp the meaning of being, although the human mind also wishes to reach a position of transcendence vis-à-vis being in order to be able to dominate it.

For Deleuze, there is no place for creativity and newness within the logic of representation. Indeed, representational thinking expresses itself in propositions that presume to represent a certain 'state of affairs', which is ultimately directed towards solutions (everything must eventually fit in a category). Moreover, this logic of representation operates through a model of recognition: something is recognized when it fits into an existing category, when there are certain similarities with other beings/events. In the words of Philip Goodchild: 'Representation thus repeats and confirms concepts, as if they were the only proper way to understand experience; it prevents any opportunity of thinking and acting otherwise'.[2]

A logic of representation thus rules over man's thoughts and life. In such a world view, the concept of transcendence consolidates the hierarchy between thinking and being; it creates categories and hierarchies between beings, and, as a consequence, Deleuze concludes that it has nothing to do with the infinite or the absolute, with newness or with creation. For him, the only possible answer to (dispose of) representation is to embrace a state of pure immanence, to think anew on a plane of immanence. And what does this plane of immanence look like, and how does it open up a space for novelty to occur?

First of all, throwing away the logic of representation means developing an allergy for dualisms and hierarchies. Immanence is therefore no longer to be seen as the opposite of transcendence; in fact, from now on, immanence has nothing to do with transcendence. The couple 'transcendence–immanence' does not even belong together: that is, for Deleuze, transcendence is merely a (negative) phenomenon that needs to be critiqued because it cannot cover the complexity of relations within being. At most, transcendence is a secondary and temporary phenomenon or effect (never a cause!) taking place purely within the plane of immanence.

According to Deleuze, immanent thought offers us the most complete understanding of reality possible, although his interest in reality in all its complexities does not make Deleuze a 'realist' in the traditional sense. Reality does not stop with the actual existing reality before us (that which has meaning, that about which something can be spoken, that which can be identified). Deleuze adds a new dimension to the actual: the virtual. Consequently, reality has two sides, a virtual and an actual one, and the virtual is as real as the actual. The most important difference between the two realms is the continuous nature of being in motion on the part of the virtual – a process of actualization, on the other hand, is a kind of *coagulation of the virtual*, the creation of a temporary, finite 'state of affairs'. The existence of the virtual is thus the primary necessity so that the actual does not fix itself into a particular logic of representation that risks reintroducing forms of transcendence. Because the virtual is necessary for 'dynamizing' (Deleuze would also say 'deterritorializing') the actual, and because it is not identifiable, quantifiable or comparable (otherwise it would be actual), one might assume that a form of transcendence slips once again into the system: indeed, does not the virtual transcend the actual? Yet Deleuze immediately refutes these assumptions, stating in fact that

> The [virtual] event might seem to be transcendent because it surveys the state of affairs, but it is pure immanence that gives it the capacity to survey itself by itself and on the plane. What

is transcendent, transdescendent, is the state of affairs in which the [virtual] event is actualized. But, even in this state of affairs, the event is pure immanence of what is not actualized or of what remains indifferent to actualization, since its reality does not depend upon it. (WP, 156)

Only from the position of an (actual) subject is the virtual transcendent because it cannot be grasped in categories. For Deleuze, however, the subject is eventually an illusion, just as any form of representation or transcendence is an illusion for him (DR, 334; WP, 49–50). Even if the subject is real, so to speak, it cannot function as a ground. The virtual, on the other hand, consists of intensities; it is a series of pure 'becomings' that are expressed within the actual and yet are separate from it. These intensities cannot be understood as objects of knowledge (they are not identifiable), and, as a consequence, the virtual can only be grasped through creative experimentation. There is not something like an 'ontological difference' between the virtual and the actual – there is a difference only in velocity or intensity: the virtual moves at infinite speed, whereas the actual wants to reduce the velocity to zero. The virtual, in other words, is the plane of immanence on which processes of actualization take place.

One could ask, of course, why the idea of the virtual is significant to Deleuze, or how Deleuze himself knows that the virtual really even exists? This last question indeed seems a matter of belief – for Deleuze does believe that if one fails to account for the virtual, one can grasp neither the complexity of the actual completely nor of reality as a whole. As James Williams formulates it, Deleuze 'attempts to show that philosophies based purely on the actual or purely on identification miss and suppress virtual pre-conditions for their own arguments. He studies actual sensations in order to deduce these transcendental conditions and he argues that a failure to account for such conditions gives an incomplete view of any actual thing'.[3]

The idea of the virtual as the 'basis' of the plane of immanence is important in this context for two reasons: first, in positing the virtual as the 'transcendental condition' for the actual, Deleuze wishes to stress that reality does not stop with actual appearances – as one could falsely assume in an immanent world view. And second, the virtual is also important from an ethical-political perspective, since it is the level where 'becomings' take place, where things come into motion and, thus, where revolution is possible (see Chapter 4).

At this point, it would be fair, however, to ask: How does the idea of immanence emerge in Deleuze's philosophy and what is its place in the history of thought in general?

The road towards pure immanence

The history of philosophy, Deleuze and Guattari write, has been one long attempt to 'install' a plane of immanence into our thoughts,[4] an attempt that has known many failures but that could eventually succeed thanks to Spinoza.

> Spinoza, the infinite becoming-philosopher: he showed, drew up, and thought the 'best' plane of immanence – that is, the purest, the one that does not hand itself over to the transcendent or restore any transcendence, the one that inspires the fewest illusions, bad feelings, and erroneous perceptions. (WP, 60)

The main problem is that people have tended to view immanence as a relational term, in its *dative* form: that is, something as immanent *to* something else. When this occurs, however, and as Deleuze is at great pains to make clear, one reintroduces the idea of transcendence. Neo-Platonism did its best to think the universe as the 'One', although it eventually elevated the 'One' to the status of a transcendent universal, instead of positing an immanent material world that can never become more than simply an attribute within the concept of the 'One'. From this point on, the battle for an 'immanence-in-itself' was irrevocably lost in favour of Christian philosophy, a trend in thought that could only bear immanence, according to Deleuze, in homeopathic doses. The plane of immanence was thus strictly controlled by a creative force of transcendence. And this was not merely a theoretical problem – as was proven by the risks that thinkers like Meister Eckhart or Giordano Bruno ran when they defended the idea of immanence too vehemently.

With philosophers such as Descartes, Kant and Husserl, the plane of immanence can be considered as a field of consciousness (the *cogito*). The rationally thinking subject is considered as 'transcendental' and not as 'transcendent', although the difference between these conceptualizations is not easy to delineate; both concepts often tend to be confused. Indeed, Deleuze discerns a certain form of transcendence present here *to which* the plane of immanence even ascribes itself (relational!). In fact, immanence is a field (a 'basin') that can receive eruptions of the transcendent and that is changed by these eruptions (WP, 46–7). The way in which this happens, moreover, is by stopping the movement. As Deleuze puts it:

> Transcendence enters as soon as movement of the infinite is stopped. It takes advantage of the interruption to reemerge, revive, and spring forth again. (. . .) The reversal of values had to go so far – making us think that immanence is a prison (solipsism) from which the Transcendent will save us. (WP, 47)

A phenomenon like 'transcendence in immanence' emerges – an idea that will become very popular in postmodern thought (and also in postmodern theology) in order to categorize the experience of the 'Other'. Salvation for this still subjugated form of immanence came from the side of Sartre, for one, who thinks the transcendental field as impersonal, and by that, 'gives back immanence its rights' (WP, 47): immanence is now no longer immanent to something else, it exists *an sich*. But the philosopher who succeeded most in barring transcendence and proclaiming the plane of immanence as the cornerstone of his metaphysics is, without any doubt, Spinoza. Spinoza represents for Deleuze the end and the peak of a development in metaphysics wherein being is thought univocally. From the theory of the univocity of being, the concept of the plane of immanence is grown. Thinking the relation of being and beings as univocal is, for Deleuze, a necessity: after all, transcendence presupposes at least a sense of bi-vocity (duality). For example, an ontology that assumes that God and His creation are two different ways of being is not univocal. This bi-vocity (e.g. as it exists in the form of analogy) enables a person to imagine one of the two poles (God in this case) as transcendent to the other pole – His creation. In Spinoza and Deleuze, however, being expresses itself in one and the same way in all beings, and this is the very definition of univocity.

The idea of univocity is thus the first step taken by Deleuze to introduce and articulate the plane of immanence within his thought. Deleuze himself traces this idea back to three moments in the history of philosophy, three moments wherein being was articulated as univocal: in the philosophy of Duns Scotus, in that of Spinoza and as found in Nietzsche (DR, 48–52). By focusing his vision upon these figures, Deleuze detects an evolution of the concept in the way that these three in particular understood univocity, with his own understanding of the term serving as a kind of culmination and apotheosis of the creativity of the trio.

Duns Scotus (1266–1308) was the first to think the relation between being and beings explicitly as univocal, though, from within a Christian framework, being still remained neutral (and, of course, as a Franciscan monk, he could not afford to be accused of pantheism!). In his case, then, all meaning and expression still needed to come from a transcendent God and not from the immanent creation. Scotus thus seemed to posit univocal being as something 'beyond' both Creator and creature.[5] Indeed, as Deleuze says, Duns Scotus merely *thought* univocal being, whereas it is only in Spinoza that being becomes fully alive (DR, 49). Despite this failure, however, Scotus made a great contribution to the development of an immanent metaphysics by 'opening up the thought of a fully univocal relation between (. . .) Life and the living that, at the same time, does not simply efface or render subordinate the differentiations between them'.[6] Indeed, as I will argue further, it is crucial to realize that univocity does not mean that all differences between beings are neutralized or relativized.

As opposed to Duns Scotus' neutral being, Spinoza introduces the term 'expression' to articulate the relation between being and beings. With this notion, being loses its neutrality (it starts to speak!): and so 'with Spinoza, univocal being ceases to be neutralised and becomes expressive: it becomes a truly expressive and affirmative proposition' (DR, 50).[7] In Spinoza, the concept of univocity becomes inextricably linked to creativity, to the infinite productiveness of being that affirms difference.

Finally, Nietzsche contributes to this univocal choir by thinking being in all its internal differentiation as a form of eternal Return (the infinite repetition of *the same difference*).[8] Indeed, in a univocal universe, the status of beings and the relation between different beings changes radically. First, how can one think the many? How are we to account for there being more than one being? In order to ascertain this situation, Deleuze sees differences *within* being:

> The univocity of Being does not mean that there is one and the same Being; on the contrary, beings are multiple and different, they are always produced by a disjunctive synthesis, and they themselves are disjointed and divergent, *membra disjuncta*. The univocity of Being signifies that Being is Voice that it is said, and that it is said in one and the same 'sense' of everything about which it is said. That of which it is said is not at all the same, but Being is the same for everything about which it is said. (LS, 179)

Second, how is this difference being thought, when being only has one voice, one meaning? Difference is now, as already suggested, thought internally, within both being and beings, as differentiations *of* being. The notion of 'internal difference' is a concept that Deleuze borrows from Bergson, who created the concept to avoid the sense of negativity that someone like Hegel introduced into his metaphysical system by defining difference as an exteriority. When this is done, difference can only be thought negatively: something differs from what it is *not*. By thinking difference internally, Deleuze however tries to unite 'the One' and 'the Many' in his thinking. Being differentiates itself through beings, so that *being is difference*. As a consequence, univocity does not equal identity, and all beings are seen to be what they are: not the same. . .

> In effect, the essential in univocity is not that Being is said in a single and same sense, but that it is said, in a single and same sense, *of* all its individuating differences or intrinsic modalities. Being is the same for all these modalities, but these modalities are not the same. It is 'equal' for all, but they themselves are not equal. It is said of all in a single sense, but they themselves do not have the same sense. The essence of univocal Being is to include individuating differences, while these differences do not have the same essence and do not change the essence of Being (. . .). There are not two 'paths' (. . .), but a single 'voice' of Being which includes all its modes, including the most diverse, the most varied, the most differenciated [*sic*].

> Being is said in a single and same sense of everything of which it is said, but that of which it is said differs: it is said of difference itself. (DR, 45)

However, the problem of the One and the Many is not always solved in a univocal manner. Aristotle, for example, against whom Deleuze positions himself in *Difference and Repetition*, derives an *equivocal* understanding of being from the being different of beings: all things *are*, but *how* they are, differs – and that difference is dependent upon *what* they are.[9] For Aristotle, beings exist in different ways because they have different essences. The voice of being sounds differently in fact through all beings. The problem with this vision, Deleuze writes, is that the specific/particular differences that emerge in this way do not touch upon the kernel of difference in itself. Aristotle does not go 'deep' enough. His notion of difference is still reliant upon a ground of identity (expressed in categories) and is therefore inadequate: 'two terms differ when they are other, not in themselves, but in something else; thus when they also agree in something else' (DR, 38). As a consequence, Aristotle is, in this case, not able to account for the possible evolution of categories (such as evolving species in biology) – 'it never shows difference changing its nature' (DR, 40). Deleuze, on the other hand, is moved by creativity, evolution and transgression: that is what difference expresses for him. The univocal definition can thus be formulated as follows: all things *are* in the same manner, independent of *what* they are. Being only has one voice – Deleuze does not stop stressing this: 'There has only ever been one ontological proposition: Being is univocal. There has only ever been one ontology, that of Duns Scotus, which gave being a single voice' (DR, 44).[10]

Univocity also implies an equality between thinking and being: what happens and what is said are one and the same thing. In this way, univocity dismisses representation by making impossible any form of pro-position. Everything is on the same level (immanence!), and as such nothing can stand out in order to assume a hierarchical position in overview of the whole, making objective judgements about it.

The idea of univocity is certainly not a new one for theologians. Thomas Aquinas (1225–74) was the one who, in the thirteenth century in his *Summa Theologica*, set out the definitions[11] that would control the theological landscape for ages – even now his authority in these matters is still tangible for many theologians, and if uncertainties or doubts arise, one can still rely on the first part (*prima pars*) of the *Summa*, questions 1 to 13, for the exact nature and formulation of the relation of causality between Creator and creature. It is indeed a common rhetoric, and also for Thomas, to explain and argue for an idea by contrasting it with its opponents. In this spirit, Aquinas wanted to articulate and defend a certain relationship between God and God's creatures (a relation of analogy) by setting it against two other positions that he judged as too extreme: equivocity and univocity. Here, Aquinas' method can help us to understand what univocity really is about and why it would be an idea that is difficult to accept for many theologians.

Aquinas, for his part, presented his position of analogy as the golden means between equivocity, which stressed the absolute difference between God and creation, and univocity, in which there was a great danger in equalizing God to all things created and by doing so, undo the hierarchy between Creator and creatures. As Eugene Thacker writes, 'For Aquinas, both the positions of univocity and equivocity go too far, one implying an absolute identity between Creator and creature, the other implying an absolute difference between them'.[12] In the case of analogy, creatures have a twofold nature: they are both earthly and divine. As a consequence, creatures are able to know their Creator, although the distance between them is too great to say that they are of the same kind. This duality disappears completely in a univocal world view. When being is considered univocally, life can be seen in its oneness. This does not necessarily mean that there is no sense of causality present anymore; it has simply become a kind of 'horizontal causality', a causality without hierarchy – precisely something that is labelled as an 'expression' by Spinoza: God expresses himself in all creatures.

It is obvious why Christian theologians were (and still are) afraid of univocity: this sounds like pure pantheism! The divine and the earthly are here combined into one single form 'that would disallow any differentiation between Creator and creature'[13] and this is precisely what Thomas was afraid of. On the other hand, taking the position of an analogy between beings also has its problems. Within an analogical world view, for example, there is also a sense of univocity, as the relationship between two creatures can be called univocal. We seem in many ways to be dealing here with two kinds of relations – and yet we struggle to discern how these relations truly relate to each other.

Duns Scotus nuances Thomas' objections against univocity so that from a theological perspective, univocity actually becomes a very interesting position. In his book *After Life*, Eugene Thacker helps us to discern how Scotus tries to show the possibilities of univocity: 'Whereas Aquinas stresses the way that univocity effaces all distinctions, Scotus will emphasize the way that univocity allows for a formal continuity between terms without simply effacing them altogether. An internal differentiation is a central component of univocity'.[14] Indeed, formally, God and beings (as modes) are equal, though their essence is not. We should not in fact confuse a formal similarity with an essential difference, Deleuze writes. 'Attributes constitute the essence of substance, but in no sense constitute the essence of modes or of creatures. *Yet they are forms common to both*' (EP, 47). God and creatures share an identity of form, 'while permitting no confusion of essence' (EP, 47).

It becomes clear now why Deleuze was so inspired by both Duns Scotus and Spinoza. He performs a 'scholastic' reading of Spinoza, thereby seeking to radicalize Duns Scotus' idea of univocity and explaining himself with the words: 'I believe it takes nothing away from Spinoza's originality to place him in a perspective that may already be found in Duns Scotus' (EP, 49).

Far more interesting than the question of the genealogy of the concept is the question as to what the effects of univocity are. With the theory of univocity, Deleuze seems to believe that a kind of 'liberation of being' has taken place in the sense that it is no longer dependent on a transcendent deity. Univocity implies an immanent world view. Indeed, univocity almost equals immanence, writes Thacker:

> If one posits a univocal relation between Creator and creature, and if this proposition means that there is something 'common' to them both, something that runs through them, then is this not an argument for a relation of immanence as well? What, then, is the difference between the concept of univocity and that of immanence? While Scotus does favor the term univocity (*univocum, univocationis*), he rarely mentions the term immanence.[15]

Other than Scotus, Deleuze explicitly states: 'Immanence is thus the new figure that the theory of univocity takes on in Spinoza' (EP, 166). And he clarifies:

> Against Descartes, Spinoza posits the equality of all forms of being, and the univocity of reality which follows from this equality. The philosophy of immanence appears from all viewpoints as the theory of unitary Being, equal Being, common and univocal Being. It seeks the conditions of a genuine affirmation, condemning all approaches that take away from Being its full positivity, that is, its formal community. (EP, 167)

In order to maximize the openings of these insights towards theology, for which I have already tried to isolate some of the most important conceptual linkages (immanence, representation, the virtual, univocity), it is now time to take a step further and draw some explicitly theological lines of thought in Deleuze's metaphysics of immanence.

Immanence and the divine life: How Spinoza makes Deleuze a theologian

In the introduction, I already suggested that it is mainly through Spinoza that Deleuze can be connected with contemporary theology. I proposed there the notion of 'life' as a pivotal concept around which all the links between Deleuze and theology might be centred. Indeed, it proves very fruitful to reconnect the idea of immanence with the central notion of this book – life. In this way, immanence is not an abstract concept but a practical 'way of life' in which thinking and being are completely intertwined. 'Actually, there is only one term, Life, that encompasses thought, but conversely this term is encompassed only by thought. Not that life is *in* thinking, but only the thinker has a potent life, free of guilt and hatred; and only life explains the thinker' (PP, 14).

Both Spinoza and Deleuze immediately relate immanence to life – and, in Spinoza's case, even divine life. 'In Spinoza's thought, life is not an idea, a matter of theory. It is a way of being, one and the same eternal mode in all its attributes' (PP, 13). While elaborating on the meaning of this connection between immanence and life, I will focus on the nature of this immanent life in order to demonstrate how both Deleuze and Spinoza show themselves as anti-anthropomorphists in that they claim that life is an impersonal affair. Moreover, I intend to highlight how living an immanent, divine life is not something that is self-evident: Spinoza, for one, discerns three stages of knowledge through which the mind has to pass before it is united with the divine. And, finally, I hope to show how this immanent life is essentially affirmative – it expresses being *as* an affirmation.

The divine life is not what Spinoza set out to describe in his *Theological-Political Treatise*; this is rather the subject of what is said about God in his *Ethics*. In the *Treatise*, the object of reflection is religion as a human artefact, an *effect* that serves to construct moral rules. 'The true originality of the Treatise is in its considering religion as an *effect*. (. . .) Even when dealing with religion, Spinoza polishes glasses that reveal the effect produced and the laws of its production' (PP, 10). Deleuze reads Spinoza as a practical philosopher, as clearly indicated in the title of one of his books on Spinoza: '*Practical Philosophy*'. Instead of interpreting Spinoza as a speculative thinker, Deleuze highlights the ethical Spinoza, even though he allows for a certain amount of speculation within this ethics. This reconnection of thinking with life or being could also be an interesting approach for theology in general: it could allow Christian theologians to once again feed their theologies upon the life of Jesus, for example. But in order to reunite thinking and being, one needs to get rid of any scheme that includes transcendence within one's world view.

So what does it mean, not only to think immanence but also to *live* it?

Immanence: A life . . .

The title of this small but visionary text by Deleuze (it was the last text he published) reveals a crucial aspect of the relationship between immanence and life. For us, life is a category we almost immediately associate with our own subjectivity and definitely when it is used in the context of philosophy. But, as has become clear by now, from the description of Deleuze's account of the logic of representation, the very idea of subjectivity is now being called into question; the subject is a figure produced by a transcendent world view. The life that Deleuze is talking and writing about is, in other words, an *impersonal* life. Deleuze borrows a concrete description of an impersonal life from the writings of Charles Dickens in order to clarify this sense further:

> No one has described what a life is better than Charles Dickens, when he takes the indefinite article as an index of the transcendental. A scoundrel, a bad apple, held in contempt by everyone, is found on the point of death, and suddenly those charged with his care display an urgency, respect, and even love for the dying man's least sign of life. Everyone makes it his business to save him. As a result, the wicked man himself, in the depths of his coma, feels something soft and sweet penetrate his soul. But as he progresses back toward life, his benefactors turn cold, and he himself rediscovers his old vulgarity and meanness. Between his life and his death, there is a moment where *a life* is merely playing with death. The life of the individual has given way to an impersonal and yet singular life, which foregrounds a pure event that has been liberated from the accidents of internal and external life, that is, from the subjectivity and the objectivity of what comes to pass: a "homo tantum" with whom everyone sympathizes and who attains a kind of beatitude; or an ecceity, which is no longer an individuation, but a singularization, a life of pure immanence, neutral, beyond good and evil, since only the subject that incarnated it in the midst of things made it good or bad. The life of such individuality is eclipsed by the singular immanent life of a man who no longer has a name, though he can be mistaken for no other. A singular essence, a life. (TRM, 390–1)

Another example of an impersonal, yet singular life is the life of a baby: pure life without subjectivity, towards which everyone is attracted and yet which itself remains completely neutral, a bundle of possibilities. The fact that life is an impersonal affair also changes our relation with immanence. Immanence is not something that can be thought. Levi Bryant formulates this as follows: 'immanence is no longer immanence to my consciousness, but rather where my consciousness discovers itself as one more element within a field of immanence'.[16] Integrated consciousness, or subjectivity, absolves in the plane of immanence. That is why the plane of immanence remains a *horizon* of thought – it would not be purely immanent (in itself) anymore if one could think it from a distance. In *What is Philosophy?*, Deleuze and Guattari devote a full page to an almost lyrical description of the difference between a concept and the plane of immanence, from which I cite here simply some pieces:

> Concepts are the archipelago or skeletal frame, a spinal column rather than a skull, whereas the plane is the breath that suffuses the separate parts. Concepts are absolute surfaces or volumes, formless and fragmentary, whereas the plane is the formless, unlimited absolute, neither surface nor volume but always fractal. (. . .) Concepts are events, but the plane is the horizon of events, the reservoir or reserve of purely conceptual events: not the relative horizon that functions as a limit, which changes with an observer and encloses observable states of affairs, but the absolute horizon, independent of any observer, which makes the event as concept independent of a visible state of affairs in which it is brought about. (WP, 36)

As I will also stress in the next chapter, the plane of immanence is not merely a neutral 'playground' of being. When Deleuze describes the plane of immanence, and contrasts it with the plane of organization, he seems to make a plea for the plane of immanence, the only plane where life as 'a' life of being can be lived.

> We should distinguish between two planes, two types of planes. On the one hand, a plane that could be called one of *organization*. It concerns both the development of forms and the formation of subjects. It is therefore, as much as one wishes, structural *and* genetic. In any case, it possesses a supplementary dimension, one dimension more, a hidden dimension, since it is not given for itself, but must always be concluded, inferred, induced on the basis of what it organizes. (. . .) It is therefore a plane of transcendence, a kind of design, in the mind of man or in the mind of a god, even when it is accorded a maximum of immanence by plunging it into the depths of Nature, or of the Unconscious. (D, 68)

Then, Deleuze gives us a description of the plane of immanence – termed here as the plane of Consistence:

> There is a completely different plane which does not deal with these things: the plane of Consistence. This other plane knows only relations of movement and rest, of speed and slowness, between unformed, or relatively unformed, elements, molecules or particles borne away by fluxes. It knows nothing of subjects, but rather what are called 'hecceities'. (...) Hecceities are simply degrees of power which combine, to which correspond a power to affect and be affected, active or passive affects, intensities (D, 68).

This looks like an adequate description of the immanent as the virtual, where the subject is replaced by a 'hecceity', an impersonal individuality through which the power of being is expressed. 'What we have in this description', Bryant says, 'which is also a description of immanence, is something akin to the fullness of being apart from all interruptions and discontinuities which the subject introduces into it by virtue of its finitude and limitations'.[17] The power of being is not immanent to our minds; it does not belong to a subject because it expresses an essence that pervades the whole of reality: it is an intensity. In *A Thousand Plateaus*, Deleuze and Guattari associate the power of being with desire. The plane of immanence is a field of desire. With their particular notion of desire, Deleuze and Guattari want to revolt against a theory of psychoanalysis that interprets the essence of desire as a shortage: desire means *not to have* something. For psychoanalytical theory, desire is generally always directed at something outside of itself, something transcendent that grants it a sense of pleasure. Deleuze and Guattari, on the other hand, want to articulate desire as a positive power in and of itself.

> There is, in fact, a joy that is immanent to desire as though desire were filled by itself and its contemplations, a joy that implies no lack or impossibility and is not measured by pleasure since it is what distributes intensities of pleasure and prevents them from being suffused by anxiety, shame, and guilt. (ATP, 172)

Immanence as a process: The three stages of knowledge

As an example of this plane of immanent desire, Deleuze and Guattari point to the Chinese Tao (ATP, 174). This indicates that immanence is associated with a dynamic life-path. This path, though, is not without its obstacles. Spinoza describes this spiritual-rational journey towards unification with God in three stages of knowledge, with each stage corresponding to different kinds of religion.

The first stage of knowledge is the state of nature, the imagination. It comprises a series of inadequate ideas because we are dealing with unstructured fantasy and impulsive sensitivity. Spinoza considers the laws of the state as an example for this kind of knowledge, because they are merely an imitation of reason (according to Spinoza). In Deleuzian terms, we could call this the level of *representation*. The second kind of knowledge is rational knowledge. It is a knowledge of general concepts. This level presupposes a gap with the first one because this level is concerned with higher, more abstract forms of knowledge that enable us to discern 'false' from 'true': 'Knowledge of the second and third kind, and not of the first, teaches us to distinguish the true from the false'.[18] The idea of God is part of this stage of knowledge: indeed, any adequate idea expresses the essence of God and brings us to the idea of God.

In Deleuze's philosophy, the transition from the first to the second kind of knowledge happens through an *encounter*. An encounter breaks through the pattern of representation and creates an awareness of (and a distance from) the actual – so that we become aware of our virtual being. Intuitive knowledge, the third kind of knowledge according to Spinoza, is the result of a leap that can only be made on account of the knowledge contained in the second kind, that of general concepts. It is the level of *beatitude*, from which love is born. At this level, my power to think and act is the power of God's self. We think like God thinks, or God thinks through us: there is practically no difference anymore between God and God's creatures. 'Nor is there any difference here, except that the mind will have had eternally these same perfections that we have just supposed to be added to it, with the accompaniment of the idea of God as an eternal cause'.[19]

Affirmation

Deleuze in fact created the concept of *affirmation* to work with this third stage of knowledge. Affirmation does not here mean an uncritical and passive acceptance of an existing situation, but presupposes that one has escaped from that situation. 'The destruction [of a representational order] without reserve creates a space for free and original creative forces'.[20] Affirmation ultimately spells liberation:

> *To affirm is not to take responsibility for, to take on the burden of what is, but to release, to set free what lives.* To affirm is to unburden: not to load life with the weight of higher values, but to create new values which are those of life, which make life light and active. (NP, 185)

Affirming life on the plane of immanence, as translated into theological terms, would be the greatest act of belief; it would be a confession of faith. 'It may be that believing in this world, in this life, becomes our most difficult task' (WP, 75).

Indeed, Spinoza explicitly connects the three stages of knowledge (we are obviously not talking about pure rational knowledge in the Cartesian sense) with different stages of religion. Existing religions still dwell on the first level – according to Spinoza, they are systems of (inadequate) signs that are translated by believers into moral directives. The second kind of religion, corresponding with the second kind of knowledge, is a religion that is not based on faith but on understanding. It is 'no longer a religion of imagination, but one of understanding. The expression of Nature replaces signs, love replaces obedience; this is no longer the religion of the prophets but, on its various levels, the religion of Solomon, the religion of the Apostles, and the true religion of Christ founded on common notions' (EP, 291). For Spinoza, the whole of philosophy is an expression of God, whereas Deleuze mostly replaces the word 'God' with 'being'. There seems to be no substantial difference between those two, so that we might conclude that Deleuze 'believes' in Spinoza's God. . . . Or even more, that Deleuze's use of the Spinozist term 'beatitude' suggests an apprehension of the 'third kind of religion', coming forth from the third kind of knowledge. On this level, we not only understand how God expresses Godself in Nature, but we are as it were absorbed in the life of God, which is an impersonal life, the plane of immanence.

Although Deleuze explicitly rejects Christian theology, Peter Hallward rightly states that his concept of being is a *theophanic* conception, according to which everything is taken to express, maybe not the God of the Christian tradition but a secularized or 'de-theologized' immanent creative force[21] – a force called God by Spinoza – and both Spinoza and Deleuze seem to start their thinking from this perspective of 'God', or of infinity. In order to be able to discern these three stages of knowledge, one has to live on the plane of immanence and, in fact, has to have reached the third and final stage, the perspective from infinity.

> Merleau-Ponty has well brought out what seems to us now the most difficult thing to understand in the philosophies of the seventeenth century: the idea of a positive infinity as the "secret of grand Rationalism" – "an innocent way of setting out in one's thinking from infinity," which finds its most perfect embodiment in Spinozism.[22] (EP, 28)

Indeed, in more theological terms, Deleuze's (and even Spinoza's) metaphysics reflect a holistic and monistic view of creation: the One (God/Being) and the many (creation/beings) are two sides of the same coin. They are related to each other through the act of expression: God expresses Himself in the whole of creation in the same way. Of course, this does not mean that everything (i.e. every being) is the same. Being is equal for everything – every being expresses the same 'amount' of Being – but not everything is equal. That is why Deleuze defines Being as *difference*, as a continuously differentiating creative force.

This view on creation can be said to correspond to *positive theologies*, and in contrast with a (nowadays popular) *negative* theology, which speaks about God in terms of what God is not. Negative theology posits a belief that God is transcendent, so that we are not able to grasp God's essence. In the words of Michael Hardt:

> Negative theologies in general affirm that God is the cause of the world, but deny that the essence of the world is the essence of

God. In other words, although the world is a divine expression, the divine essence always surpasses or transcends the essence of its expression. (. . .) The God of negative theology is expressive, but with a certain essential reserve. Positive theologies, on the contrary, affirm God as both cause and essence of the world.[23]

Avoiding anthropomorphism

Apart from the affinities that Deleuze seems to have, through Spinoza, with a positive, immanent and univocal 'theology of life', the position of Spinoza is also interesting in that it avoids being a form of anthropomorphism, even more than a theology of analogy like that of Thomas Aquinas. From this perspective, an immanent theology could be more respectful to God *as God* (and not as a projection of man) than a transcendent theology that uses an analogical epistemology to speak about God. In *Expressionism in Philosophy*, Deleuze elaborates on the hidden anthropomorphism of an analogical theology. From an analogical position, God has characteristics that humans can also have, although he possesses them eminently. God's goodness, for example, is infinite and eminent, not deducible from human goodness, but only to be pointed towards through analogy. This process contains a subtle anthropomorphism: 'it is obvious that a triangle, could it speak, would say that God was eminently triangular' (EP, 46). Moreover, the essence of beings dissolves because their complete quality (the eminent quality) belongs only to God. As a consequence, the essence of their substance dissolves too because what creatures possess formally is ascribed to the substance eminently. The power of Spinozism lies in the inversion of this problem: 'Spinoza, on the other hand, insists on the *identity of form* between creatures and God, while permitting *no confusion of essence*' (EP, 47, my emphasis). When analogy is replaced by univocity, this latent form of anthropocentrism can be avoided.

In the foregoing, I have tried to point out some key features of Deleuze's concept of immanence that might be important within the context of a discussion with theology.

To restate this first part briefly: Deleuze puts forward the concept of immanence as an alternative following his critique of representation. He wishes to move beyond the dualism of form and matter that brings with it a transcendent judgement of mind over matter. Indeed, transcendence implies a superiority of thinking over being. Deleuze wants to unify these two poles and let being speak loudly and clearly through thought and life once more. Therefore, if being is liberated from the chains of representation and we relocate ourselves on the plane of immanence, what does being say? The answer would seem to be that being necessarily only expresses Itself in all beings because being is all that there is.

So instead of asking what being says, it seems better to ask *what happens* on the plane of immanence. The verb 'happens' is indeed a better choice: everything on the plane of immanence is constantly moving, and nothing is fixed. There are no fixed identities but only intensities that move at different speeds, sometimes crossing each other, colliding with each other, then moving on. Life is impersonal, or, to use an image from the scientific field, the plane of immanence is like a field of energy in which the smallest particles are constantly moving, colliding with each other, and forming molecules that dissolve again after a while. Even these smallest particles, as quantum physics has taught, are not really stable particles but pure waves of energy.

The connection of an immanent being with life (and of transcendence with death, for that matter), immediately indicates that, for this philosopher, immanence and transcendence are not just formal categories: they are qualitative ways of understanding being that have marked consequences for the way in which we live our lives. In fact, both spiritual and ethical 'agenda' are discernable in this plea for radical immanence, showing how practically oriented Deleuze's philosophy really is.

The problem of immanence in theology and the future of immanent theologies

The theme 'immanence', when stressed too much, can indeed be considered as problematic for theology. As a lemma, it is not even present in the most famous, sound, German academic encyclopedia of systematic theology, the *Theologische Realenzyklopädie* (TRE): when one looks there for the word 'immanence', they are immediately referred to 'transcendence' for more explanation. Immanence, from a traditional theological perspective, cannot be thought apart from transcendence, or so the message seems to be. Transcendence always seems to come back into play when speaking about God. Even in Spinoza, a kind of *epistemological transcendence* can be discerned: indeed, the only attributes of God (the One Substance) that are knowable to us, are thought and extension.

Tradition appears to suggest that systems of thought are seemingly always looking for a balance between immanence and transcendence, even if most of the time, one of the terms has been stressed over the other. In Christianity, for example, God's transcendence has always been a cornerstone of its metaphysics, although one cannot deny the importance of immanence as well, especially as it is expressed through the incarnation of Christ. Another possible, and popular (and modern), way is that of Charles Taylor: he identifies immanence with the secular and transcendence with the divine. According to Taylor,[24] we live in an 'immanent frame' today, which necessarily is a 'Closed World Structure' (CWS), because it is only immanent. It cannot be critical, for it cannot escape its own, immanent position. The only solution to break open these immanent, closed structures is to allow for a transcendent reality beyond the immanent.

The (more postmodern) position of Jacques Derrida, although he still acknowledges the dichotomy between transcendence and immanence, is an example of what I think is slowly finding an entrance into postmodern theology: the idea of a 'transcendence in immanence'.

Transcendence can no longer be captivated by or within a logic of representation, and it can no longer be catapulted to another 'order' or reality (which is still the case in Taylor), that, limited as it is, runs the risk of being again represented. That which transcends us can also escape us 'immanently', Derrida seems to suggest.[25] This means that these events of *différance* stay in our midst, though not in a representable, knowable form. This form of transcendence can even be found in Deleuze, that is, if one thinks from the (albeit illusionary) dualism between the world of representation and being itself, in which being as such is not representable and thus, from the perspective of the subject, epistemologically transcendent.

For Deleuze, it is of paramount importance that transcendence not be considered as a cause – on the contrary, we need to trace transcendence back to its immanent causes: we need to think the becoming-immanent of transcendence, so to speak (see Chapter 2 for an elaboration on the process of becoming in Deleuze). Or, as Miguel De Beistegui poetically formulates it: 'Thinking with immanence, then, or thinking immanently, does not mean to eliminate all traces of transcendence. Like couch grass among flowers, transcendence grows rather spontaneously, on the back of immanence'.[26] In Deleuze's metaphysics, the 'Taylorian' dualism between the secular and the non-secular (the sphere of believers) is overcome: the immanent ('secular') becomes divine! The bottom line is that transcendence seems inevitably to be and to remain a relational term (one always has to transcend 'something'), whereas it is possible, as Deleuze tries to demonstrate throughout his oeuvre, to think immanence independently.

In theology, more and more 'immanent theologies' have begun to emerge as an alternative for transcendent accounts of the divine or those accounts in which the divine is situated in a hierarchical fashion. An immanent theology, all these theologies suggest, could pay more respect to God *as God* than a transcendent theology could, precisely because it wants to avoid the seduction of power, hierarchy and representation. From this vantage point, theologies such as those fostered in particular global contexts, liberation theologies, feminist theologies, postcolonial theologies and ecotheologies were developed from the sixties onwards in order to deal with such a false dichotomy between transcendence and immanence, and they are regaining their popularity today because the dualistic contrast of forces has not subsided with time. By way of example, I will focus on ecotheology in particular (feminist theologies will return in Chapters 2 and 4 and liberation theologies in Chapter 4).

The (mostly implicit) metaphysics behind the various ecotheologies present today is, in my view, completely compatible with Deleuze's. The core of every ecotheology, for example, is the restoration of the relationship between human beings and the rest of creation (the earth in a wide sense). There are Christian ecotheologies, but also Buddhist, Hindu, Judaic, . . . ecotheologies that share an underlying metaphysics, a common spirituality of 'sensitivity to the horizontal sacred'[27] and that all strive for a new connectedness between human beings and nature. This connectedness should not be interpreted in a new age, romantic sense; it is rather an acknowledgement of univocity present through difference: we all speak with the same voice. An overcoming of the idea of the subject is thus necessary in order to strengthen the connection between humans and non-humans. This implies a non-hierarchical, immanent view of creation. One of the 'mothers' of ecotheology, Sallie McFague, in fact defines creation as the 'body of God'. There is still room for transcendence in her world view, but she redefines transcendence in such a way that it almost becomes 'Deleuzian':

> In this body model, God would not be transcendent over the universe in the sense of external to or apart from, but would be the source, power, and goal – the spirit – that enlivens (and loves) the entire process and its material forms. The transcendence of God, then, is the preeminent or primary spirit of the universe.[28]

Divine transcendence is as it were *dispersed in the whole of creation*.[29] However, according to Luke Higgins, McFague does not go far enough in her emphasis on the immanence of the divine.

> Multiplicity and diversity are affirmed but only insofar as they can be traced back or added up to a higher, 'macrotranscendent' unity. If the divine continues to function as the guiding logic, or telos, for all that lies beneath or within it, does not the *singularity* of the *transcendent* divine consistently end up trumping the *multiplicity* of an *immanent* divine?[30]

Indeed, one might suspect a Neo-Platonist tendency in McFague's account of creation and its relation to the divine, especially in the way she still splits up the one and the many, or God and God's creatures. This emphasis places the divine again within a hierarchical, unifying position. Therefore, Higgins suggests, 'Instead of seeking the divine on the level of what we have called the macrotranscendent, what if we turn our gaze toward the smallest, most dynamic microelements of reality imaginable? What if we envision the divine not as an infinite singularity but an infinitesimal multiplicity? The divine, then, would no longer function to validate from on high a single structure or pattern of ecological relationships'.[31] This 'God in the margins' would seem to be a god in the Deleuzian sense. The *order* of the world is *not pre-given* and this 'marginal god', or 'micro-god', animates all creative becomings in the universe that is more like a *pluriverse*, to borrow a concept from Bruno Latour.[32] As I will elaborate in Chapter 3, this micro-god is a god-as-process: it influences the ecology around it but is also changed by the environment; it has a relational structure, like all healthy ecological relations. A micro-god is like the earth: it consists of fluid lava (the virtual) and a crust that is simply solidified lava (the actual). Here and there, there are irruptions where the lava lays a fertile new layer upon the crust, and new vegetation can grow. Such is the infinite dynamic of the earth.

In this way, the plane of immanence can be considered as a 'divine matrix for ecological connectedness'.[33] This matrix is not a plan, not an all-encompassing vision; it is one (one being), though it has no *telos*.

> There is therefore a unity to the plane of nature . . . This plane has nothing to do with a form or a figure, nor [sic] with a design or a function. Its unity has nothing to do with a ground buried deep within things, nor [sic] with an end or a project in the mind of God. Instead, it is a plane upon which everything is laid out, and which is like the intersection of all forms, the machine of all functions; its dimensions, however, increase with those of the multiplicities of individualities it cuts across. (ATP, 253)

Deleuze's (and Guattari's) 'philosophy of Nature'[34] provides exciting possibilities for ecotheology. The blurring of the distinction between human beings and nature[35] enables theology to think god as the absolute, as non-hierarchical, non-representable (nor visible on a macrolevel) and at the same time, as immanent. It is a god that lives *with* us, that gives us life and that we must enable to let live. Not respecting the divine relation we have with the earth only causes death. Anthony Paul Smith discerns a political ecology here, one that shows us

> that we can no longer depend on the fantasy of some stable natural law, but instead must always evaluate the relationship, asking if

this is productive of immanence or if it tends towards breaking the relationship and being destroyed by the very form of death itself. (. . .) We must decide if we are going to foster ecosystems that promote the further divergence and creation of life – what ecologists call biodiversity and Bergson called creative evolution – or if we are going to live as if we were never-living in the first place, and swallow the rest of nature up into our pure form of anthropomorphic death.[36]

Humanity has to make the leap beyond itself to form a new community with the earth, and this requires hope and belief; a belief in god as an immanent micro-process. Ecotheology has a huge task before it here, and the thought of Gilles Deleuze, as I hope to have demonstrated, provides not only a new language but also new ideas and inspirations to accomplish that task.

It is possible that the problem now concerns the one who believes in the world, and not even in the existence of the world but in its possibilities of movements and intensities, so as once again to give birth to new modes of existence, closer to animals and rocks. (WP, 74–5)

2

Spiritual life

Solus deus, utpote finis ultimus et movens primum, vivit et vita est (Only God lives and is life, because he is the ultimate goal and first mover.) (Eckhart, Lat. Werke III, 51)

The task of perception entails pulverizing the World, but also one of spiritualizing its dust. (F, 99)

For two reasons, the association of Deleuze with spirituality is not an evident one. First, as a consequence of his immanent metaphysics, Deleuze's philosophy is said to be materialist – and how can materialism possibly make a sound plea for a spiritual way of living? Despite this obvious contradiction, however, we should refrain from confusing materialism with the granting of priority of the body over the mind or some such similar proposition. According to Michael Hardt, in the history of philosophy, materialism is rather thought of as a corrective to idealism, to the priority of the mind over the body. 'This materialist correction', Hardt claims, 'is not an inversion of the priority, but the proposition of an equality in principle between the corporeal and the intellectual'.[1] Indeed, for Deleuze, thinking equals being, being *is* thinking and vice versa. Instead of speaking about materialism, it may be better to use the Spinozist term 'parallelism', about which Deleuze writes in his *Practical Philosophy*: 'what is an action in the mind is necessarily an action in the body as well, and what is a passion in the body is necessarily a passion in the mind. There is no primacy of one series over the other' (PP, 18). When Spinoza takes the body as a model of his philosophy, he therefore wants to show us that 'the body surpasses the knowledge that we have of it, *and that thought likewise surpasses the consciousness that we have of it*' (PP, 18). We could say that Deleuze wishes to save being from the (domination of the) human intellect (thinking is detached from subjectivity!), and in doing this, he perhaps creates more room for the divine, for that which escapes the control of the human intellect than a 'classical' theological, non-materialist vision that demarcates a clear space for God, namely up there, above in heaven, of whom we have knowledge only by analogy. By defining the material in terms of flows and energy (and in-line with contemporary physics), Deleuze can be said to 'spiritualize matter', or at least to appear as someone for whom the dualism of spirit and matter is dissolved in the cosmic energy of being.

Another possible objection against the characterization of a 'spiritual Deleuze' would be that he rejects any moral judgement on life in the name of immanence. Deleuze makes a distinction between morality and ethics that is very interesting in our dialogue here with theology, a discipline that traditionally has attached a high value to moral issues and judgements. Morality is a structure of transcendence: 'Ethics, which is to say, a typology of immanent modes of existence, replaces Morality, which always refers existence to transcendent values' (PP, 23). Opposed to morality then, ethics is not a system of judgement. Again, Deleuze articulates this distinction with help from Spinoza. Ethics is a process of being that happens during an encounter between two bodies: 'the good is when a body directly compounds its relation with ours, and, with all or part of its power, increases ours' (PP, 22). So ethics is a matter of productive *encounters*, not of representations. Being is ethics, increasing or decreasing the power of bodies. As a consequence, thinking is a matter of ethics too. 'There are never any criteria other than the tenor of existence, the intensification of life' (WP, 74). This suggests, as Philip Goodchild contends, 'that philosophy is less the art of judging, or of disciplining the body conform to the mind, but a formation of a "way of being or style of life". The mode of existence is the phenomenon that replaces the function of the idea'.[2] These thoughts correspond to the main idea investigated in the previous chapter, namely, that immanence is a (way of) life (PP, 122). In a sense, this chapter on the spirituality of Deleuze serves a type of preparation for living an immanent life. From the perspective of the development of thought, the content of this chapter precedes the actual work on the plane of immanence (creating concepts). 'It is the spiritual exercise that renders one capable of giving life to the idea',[3] Goodchild concludes.

The plane of immanence is thus presented by Deleuze as a *goal* to achieve, a goal that seems quasi unattainable at times because subjectivity and a tendency for transcendence continuously pop up in both thought and being. But even more of an obstacle than these temporary forms of transcendence – one that can be beaten – is the 'transcendence' of the plane of immanence itself: to live an immanent life, to give up our form of subjectivity, seems to be a goal that transcends our lives at this stage. It seems in fact to demand a whole new vision of life and a transformation of our way of living. At this point, an encounter between Deleuze and theology can be staged, and more specifically an encounter with the tradition of mysticism, the spiritual journey towards unification with God (Part II). This tradition, and *in concreto* the works of Meister Eckhart, whom I use as a dialogue partner, can show us how the radically transcendent can at the same time be radically immanent. . . . However, it is not only the Christian mystical tradition that appears to demonstrate some affinity with Deleuze's spirituality. At the end of this chapter, I will also make mention of certain Buddhist forms of spirituality as akin to Deleuze's metaphysics as well.

The result of these 'encounters', I hope, will be a better understanding of what is at stake in Deleuze's writings as well as an encouragement for religions to focus more on their mystical traditions in order to feed their theologies anew with a lively tradition of immanence and spiritual life already present within them.

Spiritual Deleuze

In the previous chapter, I interpreted Deleuze's philosophy as a practice. To live an impersonal life, that in line with Spinoza could also be called a 'divine life', appears to be an ideal for Deleuze, which one seeks to approximate with one's life. This goal provides his philosophy with a spiritual touch, and it allows his thought to become as it were visionary. I will therefore argue here that Deleuze's philosophy indeed contains a *perspective of salvation* and is thus religious, at least formally. By utilizing the expression 'perspective of salvation', I intend to show that Deleuze, in my interpretation, seeks to bring about the *liberation* of thought and life through philosophical insight into both the nature of being (and of human nature, for that matter) and the essence of reality. The concept of salvation could in this sense be interpreted generally and not necessarily connected to a Christian theology (although there are, of course, analogies between both interpretations of salvation, as I will demonstrate in the second part of this chapter).

Accordingly, I will present Deleuze's spirituality in this chapter in three parts: first, I will reflect more on the central notion of life as a spiritual concern. Whereas contemporary thinkers such as Alain Badiou, Peter Hallward and Slavoj Žižek hold the opinion that the perspective of salvation in Deleuze is merely a theoretical affair that detaches Deleuze from any kind of worldly commitment, I will try to demonstrate, by focusing on the notions of 'becoming' and 'escaping', that Deleuze's spirituality is at the same time a concrete ethical praxis – just as all famous mystics held on to the union of prayer/meditation, on the one hand, and daily work, on the other – as the recipe for a life lived closest to God (*ora et labora*). The ethical aspects of Deleuze's spirituality and its political consequences will also be further elaborated on in Chapter 4, in relation to a dialogue I there undertake with a variety of liberation theologies.

Spiritual life

Against feminist Deleuze interpreter Rosi Braidotti, who applauds the affirmative pluralism in Deleuze,[4] and against the political philosopher Michael Hardt, who underlines the political potential of Deleuze's philosophy for a radical democracy,[5] Baidou, Hallward and Žižek (among others) consider Deleuze as a spiritual thinker of loneliness, as a thinker of a 'world without others'.[6] In Hallward's opinion, this is the logical consequence of thinking difference as *singular*, meaning that difference only starts to 'work' if all specific differences (that are still based on identities) are extinct.[7] Deleuze indeed contrasts the 'singular' with the 'particular' (or the 'specific'): in both cases we are dealing with something concrete, though in the case of a singular event, the 'other' is eliminated. The singular is directed at life in general (and therefore it is universal) rather than limited to a specific living being.

The singular is, moreover, the absolute; it goes beyond any relation with something 'other' with which it would be comparable. However, all of this does not mean that Deleuze cannot think 'otherness'. For him, otherness is just not defined on the basis of his understanding of difference (e.g. as is the case with Derrida). For Deleuze, the other is related to continuity, to guaranteeing a stable world, rather than to discontinuity or interruption. Moreover, the other is not necessarily a subject or an object – the other is something more like a structure:

> The error of philosophical theories is to reduce the Other sometimes to a particular object, and sometimes to another subject. (. . .) But the Other is neither an object in the field of my perception nor a subject who perceives me: the Other is initially a structure of the perceptual field, without which the entire field could not function as it does. That this structure may be actualized by real characters, by variable subjects – me for you and you for me – does not prevent its preexistence, as the condition of organization in general, to the terms which actualize it in each organized perceptual field – yours and mine. Thus the *a priori Other*, as the absolute structure, establishes the relativity of others as terms actualizing the structure within each field. But what is this structure? It is the structure of the possible. (LS, 307)

The other immediately brings a context or a background with him/her. Deleuze defines the term 'other' on the basis of its *effects* – as he does with all concepts: the question is not what something means but *how it works*. This approach – one that seems reductive towards the other (as a subject) – is necessarily rooted in Deleuze's disdain of representation. For him, the universe is a dynamic play of intensities, not a compilation of separate identities that have their individual meaning. Separate entities that become connected and that function together in a specific way are approached by Deleuze as 'machines'. And in the case of a machine, one does not ask 'what does this machine mean?' but rather, 'how does this machine work?'

Concerning the effect of others, Deleuze writes in his *Logic of Sense*: 'The first effect of Others is that around each object that I perceive or each idea that I think there is the organization of a marginal world, a mantle or background, where other objects and other ideas may come forth' (LS, 305). The presence of others leads my attention away from that one object, one that is immediately linked by these others with other objects. The other brings with it a context or even more: the others *are* the context – a context that Deleuze describes through the words of Michel Tournier as 'a powerful element of distraction' (LS, 305): not only do the others constantly interrupt our activities and our stream of thoughts, they also enlighten a world of concerns that is situated at the margins of our consciousness but is capable of becoming the centre of our attention any time.[8] The other is (a symbol of) the surrounding world and guarantees the predictability of it.

Yet what happens when the category of the other subsequently disappears? The elements are freed from their context, from the organism in which they were held captive. A new image comes into the world, in which the elements are released and renewed. It is as if the whole earth tries to escape from the influence of others, Deleuze writes. Indeed, the other is 'the grand leveler, and consequently the de-structuration of the Other is not a disorganization of the world, but an upright organization (. . .); it is the detachment of a pure element which at last is liberated' (LS, 312–13). The activity of 'organizing' the world by the other is experienced as *wrong*,[9] and the liberation from this world (and from the other) becomes a goal.

Peter Hallward, among others, concludes from all this that Deleuze is a philosopher who wants to leave the world behind as well as the others who live in that world: 'Deleuze writes a redemptive philosophy. In conjunction with its mainly artistic allies, it is designed to save its readers from a situation contaminated by "consciousness", "analogy", "repression", "lack", and "the Other" [*autrui*]'.[10] Liberation for Deleuze means liberation *from* (ablative) the world as symbolic order or as a whole of representations.

In Deleuze's attack on everything 'worldly', worldly knowledge and worldly differences, he demonstrates – according to Hallward – similarities with the spirituality of the apostle Paul and (of course) with Spinoza. One has to die to this world in order to be reborn in the

Spirit – a Spirit that is unlimited by worldly mediations like subject and object, language and representation. The self *becomes* God as it were; it shares in the divine life, a life without otherness, without selfhood, with only intensities on a plane of immanence: 'we experience pure forces, dynamic lines in space which act without intermediary upon the spirit, and link it directly with nature and history' (DR, 12). This is also the core of Spinoza's philosophy – we are situated here on the third level of knowledge, the level on which God knows himself (see Chapter 1).

Hallward's main thesis is that Deleuze remains dependent on the world of representation in order to develop his own 'divine' standpoint. He simply appears to wipe representation away by making the actual subordinate to the virtual. In this way, Hallward interprets Deleuze as an ascetic thinker who continuously makes the movement from beings to being, who gradually withdraws himself from the world of beings.[11] Despite this critique, perhaps I can suggest that Hallward grants too much weight to the virtual. Indeed, Deleuze himself continuously emphasized that 'the plane of immanence contains both actualization as the relationship of the virtual with other terms, and even the actual as a term with which the virtual is exchanged' (D, 115). Moreover, Hallward seems to equate the actual with representations, while the actual is not necessarily captured in representations: the only difference between the actual and the virtual, according to Deleuze, is velocity: while the virtual moves at infinite speed, velocity is reduced to zero in everything that is actual. The relation between virtual and actual is thus rather complex. The actualizations that take place on a plane of immanence do not create an ontological dualism between virtual and actual, in which the virtual would transcend the actual.

Another possible critique of Deleuze's project of salvation is the apparent elitist character of this spirituality that seems to operate exclusively on the lonely level of the intellectual mind. Is Deleuzian liberation a privilege for the *aristoi* that are capable of abandoning their sense of subjectivity and becoming a 'spiritual automaton', as one imagines happens among real mystics? Though Deleuze might at times give the impression of something along these lines in some of his texts, his later works, written together with Guattari, however, are one long call to a resistance against representation, a call for 'becoming' above all else. Deleuze's writings might be rather inaccessible and demand thorough study, but his thinking is directed at the whole universe and the whole of humanity. It is my conviction that Deleuze's spiritual project of salvation needs to be complemented with a more concrete, ethical project, and therefore I will continue to discern the varied contours of those significant movements of transformation that need to be addressed in this respect: becoming and escaping.

Becoming

Nichts werden ist Gott werden (Angelus Silesius).

'Becoming' is one of the key terms in Deleuze's philosophy. Although he only develops it thoroughly in the works he writes with Guattari (especially in *A Thousand Plateaus*), the notion of *being as becoming* is already present in *Difference and Repetition* and *Logic of Sense*. Deleuze mentions the concept of 'becoming' for the first time in his monograph on Nietzsche, *Nietzsche and Philosophy* (1962), and already here, the core of its meaning is clearly expressed:

> For there is no being beyond becoming, nothing beyond multiplicity; neither multiplicity nor becoming are appearances or illusions. But neither are there multiple or eternal realities which would be, in turn, like essences beyond appearance. Multiplicity is the inseparable manifestation, essential transformation and constant symptom of unity. Multiplicity is the affirmation of unity; becoming is the affirmation of being. (NP, 24)

In other words, becoming is the ultimate reality that is *not* transcendent (there is nothing beyond appearance). Becoming is intrinsically connected to difference (multitude) and therefore, with the adagio of *Difference and Repetition* – being is difference – in the back of our minds, we understand that becoming is the ultimate affirmation of being. Everything at stake in Deleuze's philosophy becomes visible through this conceptualization of becoming: Deleuze staunchly opposes the founding of reality on a stable, static ground as is generally the traditional stance taken in Western philosophy (finding foundation in being, in God, in the reason of the subject). The ground of Deleuze's universe is a non-ground; it does not exist as such, and it is constantly moving because it *becomes*. It should come as no surprise then, that this non-ground is closely related to difference. Furthermore, becoming is a completely immanent process, taking place on the plane of immanence (that is constituted by all processes of becoming).

So far, I have spoken about becoming 'in general', a concept that as such is primarily present in the early works of Deleuze and is mostly developed therein through the thinking of Bergson and Nietzsche. It is in these earlier works as well that Deleuze writes about concrete becomings, the becoming of *something*. In *Difference and Repetition*, for example, he describes the processes of becoming-identical and becoming-mad (DR, 50–1; 178; 296). However, the most important becomings are presented in *A Thousand Plateaus*. In the following, I will try to demonstrate how all specific becomings affirm the essence of becoming 'in general' and as described above. There is something peculiar about these becomings, an aspect that is revealed as important through the tracing of a perspective of salvation within Deleuze's thought.

Upon first sight, it is not obvious at all that one should intend to look for a message of salvation within Deleuze's philosophy. Part of the originality of Deleuze's programme indeed consists in being *not teleological*: Deleuze wants to think a universe that is constantly in a state of becoming that knows neither goals nor ends (as to indicate such would only bring back a form of transcendence). Salvation will thus never be found in what one would become, as the process of becoming has nothing to do with imitating or adopting a certain identity (which is an activity on the molar or macrolevel)[12] – the redemption rather lies in the molecular (microlevel) *process* of becoming, that is infinite:

> A line of becoming has neither beginning nor end, departure nor arrival, origin nor destination; (. . .) A line of becoming has only a middle. The middle is not an average; it is fast motion, it is the absolute speed of movement. A becoming is always in the middle; one can only get it by the middle. A becoming is neither one nor two, nor [sic] the relation of the two; it is the in-between, the border or line of flight or descent running perpendicular to both. (ATP, 323)

Though the process of becoming may not have a goal, it is interesting to see how it nevertheless has a *clear direction*.[13] One does not simply become *any*thing, and not all becomings are equal or better: indeed, not all becomings are even possible. The most important becomings are those gathered under the headings of becoming-woman, becoming-minoritarian, becoming-revolutionary, becoming-animal or becoming-imperceptible. Yet, the words that accompany these becomings are at the same time a kind of restriction to that becoming.

> Why are there so many becomings of man, but no becoming-man? first because man is majoritarian par excellence, whereas becomings are minoritarian: all becoming is a becoming-minoritarian. (. . .) Only a minority is capable of serving as the active medium of becoming. (ATP, 320-1)

Becoming, as the unfolding of difference or the multitude, is clearly directed at the minority, at resistance against the State, against representation, against the (male) subject. For Deleuze and Guattari, only a minority (or 'the minoritarian') can engender a becoming. Next to its creative side, a becoming thus also has a 'deconstructive' side. The constructive aspect (the affirming of minorities as differences existing outside the world of representations) does not exist without the destruction of the order of representation or the State. In this sense, the concept of becoming is closely linked to that of escaping – with the latter being a concept that rather expresses the critical, destructive character of being (see further). Throughout their collaborative writings, Deleuze and Guattari continued to refine the direction of becomings as central to their work. All becomings, they state, begin with becoming-woman (ATP, 321) and are aimed at becoming-imperceptible: 'If becoming-woman is the first quantum, or molecular segment, with the becomings-animal that link up with it coming next, what are they all rushing toward? Without a doubt, toward becoming-imperceptible. The imperceptible is the immanent end of becoming, its cosmic formula' (ATP, 307-8).

In order to clarify the content of Deleuze's project of salvation, I will undertake a closer examination of the different aspects of these significant becomings. I will begin with the becoming-woman, and after discussing the becoming-minoritarian, I will conclude with the becoming-imperceptible. All these becomings, I should note, have great theological potential, not only if viewed from a spiritual-mystical trajectory but also within the domain of liberation theologies and feminist theologies. The sequence of becomings does not follow a definite logic, nor can they be considered as 'first becoming', 'second' and so on, Deleuze and Guattari are quick to point out. Every becoming makes connections between lines within the whole universe, though this certainly does not stop Deleuze and Guattari from maintaining preferences for certain becomings.

Where it all begins: Becoming-woman

At this point, it might be the most relevant thing simply to ask: what does this state of becoming mean? Or rather, what does this becoming *effectuate* (as inquiring after the meaning of something merely repeats the logic of representation)? If we wish to abandon the dialectical frame, Deleuze says, if we want to break free from the majority-minority opposition, we have to *become*. Becoming, as we will also see in Chapter 3, is a creative process in which something new emerges. 'To become is to become more and more restrained, more and more simple, more and more deserted and for that very reason populated. (. . .) The desert, experimentation on oneself, is our only identity, our single chance for all the combinations which inhabit us' (D, 22.9). And becoming-woman is the key to all becomings: 'All becomings begin with and pass through becoming-woman' (ATP, 306). However, the use of the word 'woman' seems – again – to affirm the man-woman dualism instead of escaping from it. But if we understand it as such, the only thing we achieve is that we are again confronted with our addiction to dualisms, to a form of difference that is opposition and that denies us access to the one being (Deleuze's sense of univocity). By positing the becoming-woman as the 'first' becoming and the condition of possibility for all other becomings, Deleuze provoked both reactions of approval as well as a certain amount of disdain from the feminist side. Why did Deleuze and Guattari actually choose woman as a point of access to the process of becoming? Becoming-woman is not an affair conducted by and for woman (although 'woman' is certainly not meant solely as a metaphor, ATP, 302). Becoming-woman does not refer to empirical women or a feminine self but to positions within society.[14] Positions of power, for example, but above all else, positions of being-minority. If one holds a minoritarian position, one does not really have a stake (i.e. meaning) within the representational order. One slips through the net, or one drops out so to speak. Precisely for that reason, Deleuze considers the minoritarian position as a way of access to being and a movement away from representational frameworks. A minority is not caught up within a hierarchical logic; it rather has the possibility of being more dynamic. As such, everyone should 'become minoritarian', according to Deleuze, though a minority should not be understood as a numerical minority. By Deleuze's count, minorities in general and women in particular do not have a model or a law by which to form themselves – they remain a process as they are infinitely becoming. Becoming-woman is therefore becoming-different, and this becoming is a line of flight beyond the coordinates of identity. The becoming, because it is a perpetual movement, engenders a continuous production of difference, an endless dynamics of transformation. Unlike many feminists (such as Luce Irigaray), Deleuze makes no plea for the creation of a female subject – as opposed to the masculine individual. Such a thing would end the process of becoming. A Deleuzian feminism is not a task of emancipation within the representational order but rather a challenge for continuous differentiation, for a state of endless becoming. As a consequence, becoming-woman has nothing to do with imitating women, but rather with the deconstruction (or in Deleuzian terms, the deterritorialization) of dominant orders of meaning like that of men, human beings, the visible, in short, of representation as a whole. The process of becoming renounces every (role) model. A striking example in this context is the figure of the 'girl', which Deleuze and Guattari mention a few times in relation to the becoming-women. For them, the girl is an experiment, she slips through all clear-cut categories and stages; the girl is not someone who becomes a woman, she is *perpetually* a becoming-woman: 'Girls do not belong to an age group, sex, order, or kingdom: they slip in everywhere, between orders, acts, ages, sexes; they produce n molecular sexes on the line of flight in relation to the dualism machines they cross right through' (ATP, 305).

From these descriptions, we can conclude that it is a 'woman' that has to accompany the process of a becoming in the first place. As all feminists will agree, a woman does not have one clearly delineated identity. In *This Sex Which Is Not One*, for example, Luce Irigaray explains how the versatility/multitude of the female subjectivity is inscribed in her body: 'Woman "touches herself" all the time, and moreover no one can forbid her to do so, for her genitals are formed of two lips in continuous contact. Thus, within herself, she is already two – but not divisible into one(s) – that caress each other'.[15] Becoming-woman is related to one's access to a world of multiplicities. A woman is as such not considered as simply the opposite of a man, not merely as 'the other': this is a new way of thinking, a new movement that is not led forward by a notion of 'identity', but by bodies, desires, streams.[16]

The concept of becoming-woman is thus part of the anti-oedipal project of Deleuze and Guattari: they want to replace the oedipal logic of psychoanalysis with a logic that is not based on identities which are founded upon a lack. Indeed, psychoanalysis considers desire as a lack *of* something. The desire of a woman, to the contrary, is not the basis for one (oedipal) identity that is modelled on the 'law of the Father'; neither can female desire be considered as a lack: it can be, and *is*, productive. Concerning sexual desire, Irigaray writes: '*Woman has sex organs more or less everywhere*. She finds pleasure almost anywhere. (. . .) the geography of her pleasure is far more diversified, more multiple in its differences, more complex, more subtle, than is commonly imagined – in an imaginary rather too narrowly focused on sameness'.[17] We must note, however, that for Deleuze, the desires that are liberated by the process of becoming are everything but the personal desires of a subject. The transformation of a becoming does not actualize *my* oppressed desires but liberates the *impersonal* power of being, life in general, something that expresses itself in that particular process of becoming.

The reasons why Deleuze and Guattari chose the figure of the woman to initiate the process of becoming provoked a fair share of critique from feminists. I want to dwell on this point for a moment because it is relevant to the consideration of Deleuze's perspective on salvation, and it will become even more significant in the last chapter on ethics and politics.

After all, Deleuze seems to leave no space for *the* traditional feminist cause: the formation of a particular female subjectivity, juxtaposed against a masculine one. He wants instead to eliminate any form of subjectivity or identity. The question for many feminists in response to this position then is, if a minimum of subjectivity is not necessary in order to have and maintain some form of political power, to initiate a transformation on a political level, how are we to fight those forms of male dominance in our lives? With the same weapons of representation, namely with an alternative subject? How else can we offer resistance? From a Deleuzian perspective, Rosi Braidotti contends, the whole historical battle of women for equality is given up.[18] For Patricia MacCormack too, becoming-woman is a concept that marginalizes women even more. According to her, becoming-woman is a concept utilized in the service of 'a male project toward alterity. Women remain, in this project, the first marker of difference and of marginality'.[19]

Still, Deleuze and Guattari do not deny the importance of a macropolitical feminist project: 'It is, of course, indispensable for women to conduct a molar politics, with a view to winning back their own organism, their own history, their own subjectivity: "we as women . . ." makes its appearance as a subject of enunciation' (ATP, 304). On a 'molar' or macropolitical level, we need a female subject. The 'molar' register concerns organisms, subjects and their interactions, the domain of the social: macropolitics. For Deleuze and Guattari, as I will demonstrate in what follows, it is the molecular, or micropolitics, that has revolutionary power. This is the level of the a-subjective being, of chemical and physical interactions and intensities. Becomings take place at the molecular level. The feminist critique of the concept of becoming-woman is thus avoided, if seen from this angle, by placing the concept on another level. Becoming-woman is not about asserting one's subjectivity, and even more, it is not about sex or gender. If Irigaray still connects the multiplicity of one's sexuality with the female sex, Deleuze and Guattari focus on multiplicities as expressions of being rather than as expressions of (and identifications with) one particular sex. 'It is badly explained by the binary organization of the sexes, and just as badly by a bisexual organization within each sex. Sexuality brings into play too great a diversity of conjugated becomings; these are like n sexes' (ATP, 307).

Yet, we should not think of the molar and the molecular as two separate levels. The infinite movement present on the molecular plane of immanence is the condition for political movement as an organization of identity or subjectivity. Deleuze and Guattari want to unveil or liberate the forgotten molecular dimension, because the transformations that take place there are much more intense: they emerge immediately from being. Becoming-woman is thus not an affair of subjects or interactions between subjects but a case of connections between intensities. Deleuze and Guattari call this the 'machines of desire' or 'assemblages'. Jerry Flieger expresses this as follows: 'Becoming-woman does not aim at the emancipation of a homogenous collectivity (women), an aggregate of same-sex subjects with a shared "identity," struggling to gain political and economic rights; it aims at tensile transformation and transgression of identity'.[20]

The 'next' step in the world of becomings focuses more thoroughly on the molecular level.

Along the way: Minorities, revolutions

The process of becoming depersonalizes the individual being more and more over time. It loses characteristics but is not less specific due to these losses. In a way, the process of becoming-woman could still be referred to certain 'characteristics' that are linked specifically to women, though Deleuze wants to rid the process of becoming of any form of representation. Becoming as such is a process that has to withdraw itself from the visible realm, that is, from the symbolic order. Hence the importance of the becoming-revolutionary and the becoming-minoritarian. The use of the word 'minoritarian' is one made on purpose, instead of the more commonly heard term 'minority', because a minority could in fact refer to a concrete group of individuals with a defined identity. 'It is important not to confuse "minoritarian," as a becoming or process, with a "minority", as an aggregate or a state' (ATP, 321). Minorities are always understood in relation to a majority. Deleuze and Guattari, however, seek to stress that the opposition between minority and majority is not a quantitative one (ATP, 116). The majority is not the group with the largest number of members; the majority rather has a constant position of power and dominance over the minority. A minority as such lacks this positioning – even if it consists of more people. 'A determination different from that of the constant will therefore be considered minoritarian, by nature and regardless of number, in other words, a subsystem or an outsystem' (ATP, 117). Only in the minoritarian position, then, can becomings take place. 'There is no becoming-majoritarian; majority is never becoming. All becoming is minoritarian' (ATP, 117). The difference between majority and minority is thus qualitative. Only minorities have creative potential (ATP, 117); only minorities are capable of bringing the majority out of balance, of 'deterritorializing' it: pulling a homogeneous system (like a majority) off its constructed path, and making it move again, making it *become* (minoritarian). In this way, becoming-minoritarian is closely connected to becoming-revolutionary. This becoming, and its relation to the development of micropolitics, will be discussed in detail in Chapter 4. In the context of this chapter, I will proceed by way of a discernment of a sense of spirituality present in Deleuze's thinking. Just such a spirituality can be found in that the process of becoming is an infinite process, as an evolution towards an ever-purer becoming, which Deleuze and Guattari describe as the becoming-imperceptible. Indeed, becoming is a return towards pure 'difference in itself', difference without identity.

The purest of all becomings: Becoming-imperceptible

> But what does becoming-imperceptible signify, coming at the end of all the molecular becomings that begin with becoming-woman? Becoming-imperceptible means many things. (ATP 308)

If becoming-imperceptible can be associated with a spiritual project, it should in any case be a project with eastern characteristics. Every time Deleuze and Guattari refer to China or to the East in general in their book *A Thousand Plateaus*, it is in the context of the process of becoming-imperceptible. Exactly what is the relation between an eastern logic (if this can be captured in one term) and becoming-imperceptible? First of all, an eastern logic is an immanent one, opposed to the eternal Western inclination for transcendence, something which they dismiss as a 'typical European disease'.[21] The East thinks in rhizomatic structures, comparable to the structure of grass, for example, as grass always, eventually wins the fight against the larger tree-like structures around it; it grows over and between everything and serves as a figure of a way out of fixed structures.[22] (The concept of the rhizome will be discussed more thoroughly in Chapter 3.)

Also in relation to the dismantling of the face – the instance that unites all aspects of a particular identity and keeps them together – the Chinese are specifically mentioned. According to Deleuze and Guattari, the Chinese are the only ones who dare to go that far: 'Cross the wall, the Chinese perhaps, but at what price? At the price of a *becoming-animal*, a *becoming-flower or rock*, and beyond that a strange *becoming-imperceptible*' (ATP, 207). Disposing oneself of one's face is part of the destruction of the logic of the signifier or the logic of representation. Everything has to become multiple as there is no longer one single face that keeps an identity together and that represents the individual (the face is thus interpreted as a form of re-territorialization – ATP, 129). 'Dismantling the face is the same as breaking through the wall of the signifier and getting out of the black hole of subjectivity' (ATP, 208). Becoming-imperceptible is not only a matter of entering the plane of immanence, in the direction of the micro-elements that escape from representational categories, it also entails a becoming-imperceptible of the *self*. 'When the face is effaced, when the faciality traits disappear, we can be sure that we have entered another regime, other zones infinitely muter and more imperceptible where subterranean becomings-animal occur, becomings-molecular, nocturnal deterritorializations over-spilling the limits of the signifying system' (ATP, 128).

The description of a domain of the imperceptible may sound a little abstract and vague – for Deleuze and Guattari, it is however very much a reality. Let us look at a concrete example: the use of drugs. According to Deleuze and Guattari, drugs enable a person to perceive things that are, under 'normal' circumstances, invisible. Under the influence of drugs, we leave behind the boundaries of representation, lose our subjectivity and are absorbed as it were by the stream of becomings. Only the elements of a becoming are present: 'They are distinguished solely by movement and rest, slowness and speed' (ATP, 280). Movements are indeed imperceptible. Of course, Deleuze and Guattari do not wish to make an ordinary plea for hallucinatory experiences through the use of drugs. They mention in fact that drugs can initiate a deterritorialization, but they can also and at the same time hinder us tremendously on other levels, by making us dependent (addiction), for example, to the dose or to the dealer (ATP, 313–14). The example of drugs, though, also clarifies another aspect of the becoming-imperceptible. Drug addicts often admit that, although they initially started using particular substances in order to be or to feel special, they become more 'like everyone else' through their addiction: they lose all of their unique characteristics, their 'properties' as it were. Apart from the addiction, this ability to 'become-anybody' is a kind of becoming-imperceptible because it is a form of the dissolving of identity. When Deleuze and Guattari therefore formulate this approach, it almost sounds like a spiritual assignment of sorts: 'If it is so difficult to be "like" everybody else, it is because it is an affair of becoming. Not everybody becomes everybody [and everything: *tout le monde* – Trans.], makes a becoming of everybody/everything. This requires much asceticism, much sobriety' (ATP, 308). It is similar to traditional Chinese art, they add, for it is not about imitation or structure; it is instead a cosmic process in which one act, painting a fish, *becomes* the movement of the fish.[23]

If the process of becoming reaches its point of culmination in the becoming-imperceptible, we have to conclude that, although the concept of 'becoming' sounds as if it is affirmative, the effect of a becoming eventually entails a destruction or disappearance of the subject and its characteristics. At the same time, however, this destruction of a representational logic and its accompanying subject also spells out the affirmation of another universe – though it is no longer an 'I' that affirms this universe. . . . For this reason, the concept of becoming and that of escaping are closely related.

Escaping

Apart from the concept of becoming, the concept of escaping also seems to support a dialectic between the symbolic order of representation and a universe beyond it. I connect this dialectic (which is, for Deleuze, an illusionary one because representation is an illusion) with a particular perspective on salvation, in the sense that Deleuze makes a convincing decision for a world outside of representation; that is, he makes a choice that depends on the realization of a completely different ontology or world view. Deleuze himself absolutely detested any form of dialectics and tried to avoid them at any price. In relation to the above-mentioned dialectic between the symbolic order and pure being, Deleuze would reply that, for him, the symbolic order is a part of being. This order is a temporary but inevitable 'reterritorialization': the free moving lines of intensity through which being expresses itself and which have temporarily formed a conglomerate in which certain codes rule. Deleuze also calls this phenomenon *stratification*. 'Strata are Layers, Belts. They consist of giving form to matters, of imprisoning intensities or locking singularities into systems of resonance and redundancy, of producing upon the body of the earth molecules large and small and organizing them into molar aggregates' (ATP, 45). Reterritorialization is an inevitable phenomenon, though, at the same time, Deleuze's books bubble over with concepts created to liberate us from this coding, these processes of giving meaning and fixing it semi-permanently. 'Stratification in general is the entire system of the judgement of God (but the earth, or the body without organs, constantly eludes that judgement, flees and becomes destratified, decoded, deterritorialized)' (ATP, 45). Not only is deterritorialization the basis or the condition for every reterritorialization, Deleuze and Guattari compare strata to the judgement of God. To say as much is to construct a reality in which a form of transcendence has entered and infected our being again, preventing being from expressing itself freely, from in fact living freely.

Not only does becoming go in the direction of the imperceptible (away from dominant discourses and positions), escaping too implies a movement in a well-defined direction. For Deleuze, deterritorialization is a movement caused by lines of *flight* that express the multiplicity of being (ATP, 36). The expressions used by Deleuze and Guattari also therefore suggest, so it would seem, a certain preferential directionality.

> You make a rupture, draw a line of flight, yet there is still a danger that you will still reencounter organizations that restratify everything, formations that restore power to a signifier, attributions

that reconstitute a subject – anything you like, from Oedipal resurgences to fascist concretions. Groups and individuals contain microfascisms just waiting to crystallize. (ATP, 10)

Stratification or reterritorialization are described in this citation as a danger – the neutrality of a temporary but necessary movement seems to have disappeared.[24] Perhaps Deleuze's turn towards being, one that makes any kind of dialectic superfluous, did not succeed a hundred percent. And we might therefore wonder whether or not he went far enough in affirming being. Is there – at least in his vocabulary – still room for a battle between a positive sense of being and the negative logic of representation?

From the foregoing analysis, it is possible to make some conclusions concerning the specific character of Deleuze's thinking. I previously sketched an overview of those important aspects of his thought that could be formed into a sort of visionary programme, a philosophy with a particular perspective of salvation, in the sense that it proclaims liberation from a representational logic. Through his works, Deleuze makes a double trace with this liberation: on the one hand, the way towards pure being is a spiritual project, in which true life can be reached if we see and live the complexity of reality as it is. Not in terms of identities, organizations and institutions but in terms of intensities, velocities and power. In the words of theologian Anthony Smith:

> The spiritual elements in Deleuze's philosophy are located in the givenness and creation of realities that exist at the sub- and supra-individual level; these realities may not be represented adequately through molar identities, but can only be experienced as the immanence of these realities themselves.[25]

On the other hand, the project of salvation also contains a concrete task: we are all called to become imperceptible and resist the world of representation from a minoritarian position. Deleuze's salvation is also consequently to be seen as a form of political salvation – albeit on the microlevel, as I will explain in Chapter 4. Here, I solely wish to make some connections between Deleuze and different spiritual theologies in order to unveil the transformational power of both Deleuze's spirituality and these already established theological viewpoints.

Becoming-divine with Meister Eckhart and the Chinese

Becoming-divine is not a becoming that Deleuze himself describes; the concept comes from the French feminist philosopher and psychoanalyst Luce Irigaray and was picked up by one of the most famous feminist theologians of the past century, Grace Jantzen (1948–2006). The idea of becoming divine as a task for men and women is not widely accepted among all feminists; the opponents either believe that religion in general has already caused enough damage for women or they contend that 'too many men have done far too much damage acting as though they were godlings for feminists to have much appetite for the role'.[26] With the concept of becoming divine, Irigaray imitates the way in which the image of God has always worked in history: as the mirror of the symbolic order. God as the Divine Father possesses the highest qualities (omnipotence, omniscience, goodness, . . .) and serves as an ideal for men, something after which they try to shape their subjectivities. How do women relate to this male ideal? 'According to Lacan', Grace Jantzen writes, 'to the extent that women take up subject positions, entering into the symbolic, the discourse of western civilization, to that extent women also become masculinized. Either we learn to play men's roles by men's rules, or else we take up the "feminine" roles of motherhood and service structured for us by men'.[27] It is thus Irigaray's (and Jantzen's) aim to enable women to develop their own subjectivity, according to their own 'god' who functions as a horizon, an 'ideal of wholeness to which we aspire'.[28] At first sight, Deleuze would certainly not support this project of 'mimicry' in which women merely imitate the methods of men to become subjects next to them. We need to take a closer look, however, at what Irigaray and Jantzen mean through their use of the expression 'divine', what the goal of this becoming divine precisely is. On the one hand, Irigaray writes that 'divinity is what we need to become free, autonomous, sovereign'.[29] In these terms, becoming divine appears as a struggle for power, a macropolitical feminist battle in which God serves as both the motivator and the goal. And I think it is, and necessarily so, in some respects.

There is another aspect, however, upon which it is interesting to focus. God is not an omnipotent super-being for her, but 'a name to describe the possibilities of awareness, and transcendence'[30] – transcendence here understood as a type of 'horizontal transcendence', indicating an overcoming of static subjectivities. Feminist thinker Elisabeth Grosz describes the divine in Irigaray as a 'field of creativity':

> For Irigaray, the divine is not simply the reward for earthly virtue, all wishes come true; it is rather the field of creativity, fertility, production, an always uncertain and preempted field. It is the field or domain of what is new, what has not existed before, a mode of transcendence, a projection of the past into a future that gives the present new meaning and direction. The divine is a movement . . . a movement of love. . . .[31]

Becoming divine as the process of living a free life on a constantly moving field of creativity – what could this mean in a theological context?

To find a connection point for further dialogue, I want to move towards the heart of every theological and religious tradition, namely, the mystical encounter. The mystical heart of a tradition is the place where unification with the divine is experienced, the heart that nourishes a religious tradition, but that is, at the same time, quite marginal within that tradition, especially in the sense that what is at stake in the mystical experience cannot be represented. Mysticism, in short, is about avoiding the logic of representation. Moreover, 'tradition' has often looked suspiciously at its own mystics and mainly because the idea of one's unification with God has appeared to threaten His transcendence and sometimes even seemed to resemble certain heretical positions, such as pantheism. In other words, these mystical trends in thought might serve as ideal conversation partners with Deleuze.

The concrete partner in this chapter will be Meister Eckhart (*ca.* 1260–1327), someone, of course, not chosen coincidentally: although there are important ways of divergence, Eckhart's thoughts (implicitly) show important affinities with Deleuze's philosophy. By bringing these two great minds together, I want to try to understand better the spiritual aspirations of Deleuze's project (in confronting them with reports of spiritual experiences), and, on the other hand, to show the relevance of Eckhart today, especially in the context I have here created, the context of a search for a theology that resonates with (some of) Deleuze's spirit – that which would be an immanent theology of life.

Finally, I will make a short excursion to Buddhist spirituality in order to indicate important affinities with Deleuze and this tradition as well. There is a lot of material concerning the link Deleuze-Buddhism to be investigated, and I can only point towards some interesting similarities in both world views that would also perhaps be of interest to many in the Western world, knowing that Buddhism and the way of life it proclaims still have a significant rate of popularity amongst postmodern, Western faith-seekers. Although no Buddhist 'theology' really exists, there being no 'God' in Buddhism, many Christians today in the West turn to the Buddhist legacy in order to revive their own spirituality.

Eckhart and the voice from eternity

'He spoke from eternity', Johannes Tauler said of Eckhart, soothing the latter's many readers who had difficulties understanding what he was writing about. Because of his strong belief in (and high demands of) the possibilities of the intellect to reach, or better, to receive God, Eckhart is not always lucid to his readers. 'Whoever doesn't understand this speech, shouldn't care about it. For as long as man does not equal truth, he will not understand these words',[32] Eckhart writes. Thinking is eternal and, therefore, it cannot be created. The same counts for God, and that is the reason why Eckhart associates God and thinking (at first) with non-being. It is with our capacity for thinking, then, that we are able to become formally identical to God. Our mind is our access to God. Eckhart expresses himself as a thinker of equivocity – there seems to be a radical distance and difference between God or non-being and creation (being). He firmly rejects the idea of a Thomist analogy, as there is to him, no common ground between God and creation.

In his later writings, however, Eckhart identifies being and thinking as taking place *in* God. What changed over time was his broadened understanding of being: being is no longer dependent on substance, it can be more than that. The scheme is turned upside down: God is being, creatures are nothing. *Esse est Deus*, being is God, is the new adage of the later Eckhart, although the divine being remains independent from created beings. The being of beings does not exhaust God's being. (This even makes sense from a Deleuzian, materialist perspective: everything comes forth from the virtual, and goes back to it; the actual is 'only' a temporary coagulation of the virtual.)

How then, can creatures receive God in their minds? Is there any way in which a creature, who is nothing, can come into contact with being? Is there a point where two apparent opposites can meet, where equivocity becomes univocity and where hyper-transcendence touches the purely immanent? Or in Deleuzian terms, how does the process of counter-actualization take place?

It turns out that, for Eckhart, the two extremes can come very close to each other.

When a human being detaches himself from his own identity, an emptiness is freed, creating a space that can now be occupied by God. Eckhart, being called not only an academic *Lesemeister*, but also a *Lebemeister*, being a charismatic preacher and a teacher of life, makes plea for an *ethics of being* beyond concrete laws and prohibitions that want to control people's acts. An attitude of becoming-empty of oneself (dare we write becoming-imperceptible?) expresses the core of this ethics: the imitation of Christ (*imitatio Christi*). In completely effacing oneself at the service of one's neighbour, one not only becomes like Christ, *one becomes Christ*. Rather, *we* disappear, and Christ takes 'our' place. Becoming-imperceptible thus, from this point of view, equals becoming-Christ!

How is this becoming portrayed? Unlike other mystics, Eckhart does not describe the way towards unification with God in clear and marked stages. It is a journey, but the journey consists exactly of leaving behind any form of coordination or representation, so that everything starts to move and everything is perceived as something new. This way leads us to the *Grunt* (ground) where we are empty and ready to receive God, up to the point that Eckhart states that God's ground is my ground: 'Here God's ground is my ground and my ground is God's ground. Here I live from my own, as God lives from His own.'[33] On the ground, equivocity meets univocity. And this ground is not something abstract – to the contrary, it is the very concrete bottom on which we walk, the earth to which we fail to pay attention because we presuppose it – it is evident, fundamental, omnipresent; it is one and many at the same time.[34]

And do we find a trace here of what Deleuze calls the *plane of immanence*? Indeed, Eckhart-interpreter Bernard McGinn confirms that 'on the deepest level, that of fused identity, there is only one univocal *grunt*'.[35] In order to reach it, we have to leave behind all forms of representation, all images and our personal sense of subjectivity. The identity of the human being with God that is reached on the ground, should not be understood as a static identity. In McGinn's words again: '*Grunt*, therefore, should be understood not as a state or condition, but as the *activity* of grounding – the event or action of being in a fused relation'.[36] Eckhart himself advises, according to sermon 39 (ed. Quint): 'Enter into your own ground and work *there*: the works that you perform *there* are all living'.[37] As such, Eckhart's hyper-transcendent God can actually be found in the purest form of immanence, namely in a human being who is completely detached from all 'images' and finds himself or herself on the 'ground'.

Indeed, one of the most important concepts within Eckhart's writing is that of '*Abgeschiedenheit*', or detachment. The emptiness or the nothingness of which Eckhart speaks, is not God's being-nothing but creatural nothingness: the creature makes room for the fullness of God. From this perspective, Eckhart is, in the words of McGinn, rather 'the man from whom God hid nothing'[38] than an apophatic theologian and rather a hidden pantheist than a negative theologian.

Eckhart's and Deleuze's metaphysics share, we might say, the same 'spirit'. It is ruled by the same dynamic of 'becoming nothing' (Eckhart), or 'becoming imperceptible' (Deleuze), and by the urge to let go of the 'image of thought', of the illusion of identity. Eckhart's sermons speak for themselves:

> Go right out of yourself for God's sake, and God will go right out of Himself for your sake! When these two have gone out, what is left is one and simple.[39]

In as many words, Eckhart explicitly denies the use of a model of analogy to think the relation of the creature with God. God expresses

Himself in a similar way in all creatures: this is what is called univocity. In the following fragment, we can see how close equivocity and univocity approach each other: the soul – or the mind, our very capacity to think – is uncreated, just as God is, and, as such, it has the capability of becoming equal to God. Eckhart makes room for the transcendent God to become immanent through the *Grunt*.

> Saint Paul left God for God: he left everything that he could get from God, he left everything that god could give him and everything he might receive from God. In leaving these he left God for God, and *then* God was left with him, as God is essentially in Himself, not by way of a reception or a gaining of Himself, but rather in an essentiality which is where God is. [. . .] as I have said before, there is something in the soul that is so near akin to God that it is one and not united. It is one, it has nothing in common with anything, and nothing created has anything in common with it. All created things are nothing. But this is remote and alien from all creation. If man were wholly thus he would be wholly uncreated and uncreatable. If everything that is corporeal and defective were to be comprehended in this unity, it would be no different from that which this unity is. If I were to find myself for a single instant in this essence, I would have as little regard for myself as for a dung-worm.
>
> *God gives to all things equally, and as they flow forth from God they are equal*: angels, men and all creatures proceed alike from God in their first emanation. To take things in their primal emanation would be to take them all alike. [..] *All things are equal in God and are God Himself.*[40]

Everything 'flows forth' (*exitus*) from God, and all creatures 'flow back' (*reditus*) into the divine which is their essence: such is the *metaphysics of flow*, as McGinn discerns it in Eckhart's texts.[41] Although this metaphysics is clearly influenced by Neo-Platonic thought (which holds on to the distinction between the One and many creatures, their connection only being established through emanation), it is also possible to recognize Deleuze's dynamic of the virtual/actual in it, a dynamic taking place on the ground, in the plane of immanence.

Only when individuals let go of their identities (*reditus*), can God 'be Himself' in them (*exitus*).

SPIRITUAL LIFE

That this is a highly demanding, spiritual way of living, is also clear for Eckhart. One must live beyond mere purposiveness and must leave the world of representation and identity behind.

> The man who is established thus in God's love must be dead to self and all created things, paying as little regard to himself as to one who is a thousand miles away. That man abides in likeness and abides in unity in full equality, and no unlikeness enters into him. This man must have abandoned self and all this world.[42]

To live an ethical life means, in the first place, finding God in the deepest parts of your soul. This search for God is hard work. But when you have found God inside yourself, then every act you perform, expresses something of the divine life:

> If God is to make anything in you or with you, you must first be reduced to nothing. Therefore enter into your own ground and work *there*: the Works that you perform *there* are all living. [. . .] If it happens that *God* prompts you from without to work, in truth, all *those* Works are dead. For your works to live, God must prompt you in the inmost part of your soul, if they are to live, for there your life is, and there alone you are living.[43]

Of course, Eckhart is not the Deleuze of the thirteenth century. There are many obvious differences between the two thinkers.[44] Whether it was the *Zeitgeist* or his genuine conviction, we will never know, but Eckhart was sometimes closer in his metaphysics to a form of equivocal Neo-Platonism than to a univocal immanentism. (Deleuze himself suggests that bringing in more immanence in his system would perhaps have been too dangerous for Eckhart during his time,[45] and indeed, Eckhart is the only well-known mystic of whom part of his writings were condemned by Rome. . .) . Moreover, Deleuze never equalized being with Love, as is a core thought of Eckhart's – or could the equation of being with affirmation be compared to a cosmic kind of love. . . ? In any manner, in Eckhart's work, theology, philosophy and spirituality are boldly intertwined in such a way that is not evident for a postmodern, enlightened reader, although this intertwined nature also characterizes Deleuze's thought. With this (far too) short juxtaposition of their metaphysics, I want to demonstrate that Deleuze's model of immanence is not as a-religious as might seem upon first sight. His philosophy is indeed a practice towards real Life. At the same time, I hope to have suggested that Eckhart's writings are still very interesting for a contemporary theology that wishes to renew itself by bearing witness to a univocal world view and to an immanent god.

Deleuze's spirituality as a philosophical foundation for Buddhism

By finally focusing briefly on Buddhism, I do not want to simply 'compare' both Deleuze's and a Buddhist's vision on life. Neither will I investigate the words of the Buddha in detail nor study a Buddhist author in order to look for Deleuzian aspects in his metaphysics. In spite of these limitations, I want to make a connection between Deleuze and Buddhism for two reasons: first, the connection should help to clarify the spiritual aspect of Deleuze's thought on a deeper level. On the surface, Buddhism seems to be a more evident partner for dialogue than Christian mysticism because of the absence of a personal God and because it is a worldview based on 'insight' and not on an act of faith.[46] Second, I think the link might help us to make a theological evaluation of the 'spiritual Deleuze' as well as a Deleuzian evaluation of the role of spirituality in theology.

Deleuze's way of thinking is an unconventional one: for him, thinking has little or nothing to do with rational argumentation. He calls it (using a Bergsonian term) an 'intuition' or a 'creation' and uses a form of radial empiricism that could also be ascribed to Buddhism: it is about an openness towards experience that is also envisioned through the Buddhist practice of meditation (however, neither Deleuze nor practicing Buddhists would call this sensual and spiritual openness an aim or a result of meditation; they would rather speak of an *effect*). This awareness (or mindfulness, to use a popular term) is the first step in the dissolving of the subject: 'focused awareness is difficult not because we are inept at some spiritual technology but because it threatens our sense of who we are'.[47] The activity of meditation enables us to perceive with our senses a constant stream, a stream of colours, shapes, tastes, textures, ideas.[48] Neither Deleuze's concepts nor the teachings of Buddhism (*dharma*) offer ready-made answers to the questions and problems of life. According to Deleuze, the task of philosophy is the creation of problems and subsequent experimentation with them. *Dharma*, too, is not a system of answers; 'It is a method to be investigated and tried out'.[49] In that sense, both ways of thinking are an experimental practice, a way of life, rather than a system of abstract theories.

Deleuze himself sporadically refers to affinities with Zen Buddhism and with Buddhism in general.[50] He thinks that 'we really do lack in general a particle of the East, a grain of Zen' D, 67). In *Logic of Sense*, he writes that he wants to sketch an image of philosophy that is one-third Zen and, in *The Fold*, Deleuze refers to the Japanese origin of the concept of the event (LS, 248; F, 120). The many references to China in *A Thousand Plateaus* in the context of becoming-imperceptible, which I have already mentioned, are not to be neglected of course. Moreover, Deleuze often refers to 'the Orient', or 'the eastern logic' in relation to his own rhizomatic thinking (I will discuss the figure of the rhizome more thoroughly in Chapter 3).

The giving up of the subject, the rejecting of the world of representation as an illusion, the acceptance of an immanent world view in which there is no room for a transcendent cause of God, and the construction of philosophy as a lived practice, are all very Buddhist-like characteristics. 'Insight in an impersonal life' is a line that could typify both Deleuze's thought and Buddhism. Let us focus for a moment on the impersonal aspect of both 'ways of life'. Instead of speaking about a 'loss of identity' or a 'giving up of the subject', Buddhism teaches us that this process should be interpreted positively: indeed, it is rather about the 'discovery' that *there never was a subject or a self*. It is about a (re)discovery of the way in which reality works, an awareness (the Buddhist 'Nirvana', the Deleuzian 'liberation') that the subject is an illusion.

Bearing witness to a holistic spirituality, it is moreover possible to connect Deleuze with many forms of spirituality. However, this 'multifunctionality' does not mean that Deleuze's philosophy is a noncommittal affair that can be used for almost any spiritual purpose.

It might even appeal to the very core of the Christian 'catholicity' (Rom. 2:29), as Leonard Lawlor suggests:

> Not being restricted to ethnicity, not being restricted to a part, it crosses borders toward the whole (*kata-holos*); in fact, maybe Christianity concerns nothing but border-crossings. In the event of Christ, God crosses the border of the human. Crossing this border, God is not reduced to man, to the actual; the incarnation is not a mere negation of God; it is not pure negativism. Here, we would need to open a discourse of 'theology' (a discourse of the divine) and not theology (a discourse of God).[51]

The result of such a 'catholic-Deleuzian' reflection on Christianity would result in what Lawlor calls 'life-ism':

> Life itself becomes the background or ground for all other oppositions. This shift to the level of ground implies that the traditional problems associated with the concept of life are pushed to the side, problems such as the unity of life (vegetative versus cognitive), the specificity of life (organic versus inorganic), the opposition between finalism and mechanism, the conceptions of evolution. Instead, replacing being as well as nature, life becomes *ultra-transcendental*. (. . .) We can assemble the characteristics that define the new concept of life. It would not be biological in a strictly material sense; it is not natural life (*zoon*). Instead, this life, this living, is spiritual. To call life spirit (as opposed to matter) implies conceptualization, information, the virtual, memory.[52]

Nowadays, spirituality is an affair of the individual searching for the meaning of life. Deleuze reminds us that spirituality is not about our own subjectivity: quite to the contrary. He gives us a contemporary language to understand that spirituality is about transcending our subjectivities, about *relating again* to the divine existence that is life itself. Deleuze's spirituality is thus a relational spirituality, directed at a 'new earth', a new community (WP, 109). As already indicated, mysticism is not detached from ethics, an insight also of paramount importance to Eckhart.

Despite the Christian tendency to praise a *vita contemplativa* above a *vita activa*, great mystics such as Eckhart have always contested this distinction. In his sermon on Martha and Mary, the sisters from Bethany, Eckhart protests against the accepted interpretation that Martha, with her practical concerns, leads a 'lesser' life than her sister Mary, who has developed a finer spiritual life. For Eckhart, to the contrary, it is Mary who is only at the start of her development, while Martha is actually much further. The biblical verse that ascribes to Mary 'the best share' (Luke 10:41–2) is turned completely upside down by Eckhart: 'That is why Christ spoke to her and meant: "Don't worry, Martha (also) she has chosen the best share. This [meaning Mary's inactivity] will disappear with her [. . .] she will become as glorious as you!"'[53]

In Deleuze, being as such replaces the subject as 'subject', or rather, being enables us to become *who we really are*: intensities of being that express the dynamics of being. Deleuze makes the transition from the individual to the one being: (Deleuze cites Bergson's *La pensée et le mouvant*) 'Instead of diluting his thought in the general, the philosopher should concentrate it in the individual. . . . The object of metaphysics is to recapture in individual existences, and to follow to the source from which it emanates, the particular ray that, conferring upon each of them its own nuance, reattaches it thereby to the universal light' (DI, 25). With this task, the philosopher is very close to the mystic; and so, Deleuze refers to a domain beyond representation that, from the representational perspective, remains a mystery: 'At the limit, it is the mystic who plays with the whole of creation, who invents an expression of it whose adequacy increases with its dynamism' (B, 112).

3

Creative life

*By its existence alone, the lily of the field
sings the glory of the heavens, the goddesses and gods.*
(DR, 96)

There is no other truth than the creation of the new.
(C2, 146–7)

As mentioned in the introduction, this chapter serves as a kind of hinge between the first two chapters and the last one. By producing a meditation on the meaning, or rather on the *function* of creativity in Deleuze, as well as on the question of how such a thing could affect a theological notion of creation and creativity, we will be able to make the transition from metaphysics to ethics. The distinction between those two is, however, from a Deleuzian perspective, rather artificial; for Deleuze, as for Spinoza, metaphysics equals ethics. It is precisely the notion of creativity that explicitly connects metaphysics to ethics (in the broadest sense, as a 'way of life') because it indicates the fact that philosophy is not a static enterprise: it moves continuously, constitutes problems, or questions, and creates concepts around them. An essence is therefore not something to be reflected upon a posteriori; it is to be constituted in an act of creation (Spinoza would say moreover that essences are constituted by the attributes that express them). Metaphysics is thus intrinsically linked to production, creation, an invention of the new – and thereby to concrete life.

The traditional, theological definitions of creativity and creation are radically rethought by Deleuze: 'the search is not for an eternal or universal, but for the conditions under which something new is created (*creativeness*)' (TRM, 309). While creativity in the theological sense has always been connected to the given creativity of God (and as demonstrated in his creation), Deleuze pulls creativity out of its static status of givenness in order to enable creativity to *work* again. Creation, in that sense, would not be the expression of God without its also constituting (creating) God at the same time. Creation, in other words, is not an activity of a transcendent event which is passively undergone by all that is immanent; it is the immanent dynamic of being itself. (This dynamic is perhaps more akin with another theological idea of creation, namely the sense of a continuous creation or *creatio continua*, as I will explain in the second part of this chapter.)

In his account of creation and creativity, Deleuze leans heavily upon the philosophies of both Bergson and Nietzsche. I will not discuss the influence of both thinkers on Deleuze in depth, however, as the focus I want to look at lies within the possible consequences of an interpretation of being and thought as forms of creativity for theology. Bergson, Nietzsche and others will appear in this discussion only if they prove useful for the clarification of my argument. Bergson, for example, provides the link between creativity and the virtual – whereas Nietzsche connects creativity with repetition (the 'Eternal Return'). In my overview of creativity in Deleuze, the concepts of the virtual and repetition will become very significant, especially when viewed next to the figure of the rhizome. These aspects will then return in the discussion of particular theologies of creation and creative theologies. In this and the next chapter, the full potential of the philosophy of Deleuze for theology will become clearer: it is indeed possible; I will try to demonstrate, to develop a *constructive, positive theology* 'after Deleuze'.

Creative Deleuze

After giving a general account of the concept of creativity in Deleuze's work, I will develop three important and indispensable characteristics of creativity in Deleuze: virtuality, the rhizome, and repetition.

For Deleuze, being is creativity. The act of creation is also known as *differentiation:* it is the way in which being expresses itself. 'Differentiation is never a negation but a creation, (...) difference is never negative but essentially positive and creative' (B, 103). This quote is the expression of the core of Deleuze's metaphysics, and with Bergson, he defines difference essentially in a positive way. How does Deleuze escape Hegel's solid system, in which difference is thought through a negative movement of being, with the difference between being and nothing as an *Ur*-difference? For Deleuze, the difference that emerges through a negative movement of determination is a false notion of difference. A difference achieved through determination is always based on an exteriority, that is, on something outside of the differing objects (e.g. a sensual perception). Deleuze's difference is not a contrast within being but part of the dynamic of being itself. Again following Bergson, the sense of difference that is thought by Deleuze is an *internal* difference. This means that being naturally diversifies, that it is involved in a perpetual act of creation. Internal difference means that a thing immediately differs in the first place from itself, while in Hegel's philosophy, a thing differs in the first place from what it is *not* (DI, 42). 'However, instead of something distinguished from something else, imagine something which distinguishes itself' (DR, 36). This internal difference is, according to both Bergson and Deleuze, the 'explosive internal force that life carries within itself' (DI, 40). Bergson calls this the *élan vital,* and it is, indeed, pure creativity. Being is difference, and difference founds being,[1] and thus we can conclude that being *is* creativity.

From a theological point of view, this is a very revolutionary standpoint. Creativity is thought immanently from this perspective as there is no one transcendent creator; to the contrary, our task is to 'liberate man from the plane or the level that is proper to him, in order to make him a creator, adequate to the whole movement of creation' (B, 111). Creativity henceforth becomes an immanent and impersonal process that is infinite and knows no beginning or an end. The idea of creation occurring out of nothing (*creatio ex nihilo*), the doctrine by which theology has historically wanted to testify to God's power and greatness, is thus nonexistent within Deleuze's creative universe. In his *Creative Evolution,* Bergson formulates these thoughts as follows:

> Everything is obscure in the idea of creation if we think of *things* which are created and a *thing* which creates, as we habitually do (. . .). There are no things, there are only actions. (. . .) God thus defined has nothing of the already made; He is unceasing life, action, freedom. Creation, so conceived, is not a mystery; we experience it in ourselves when we act freely.[2]

'There are no things, there are only actions' is an interesting thesis that comes about as the consequence of Bergson's two ways of being. As such, he is able to distinguish between a virtual being and an actual being. The dynamic process of creation, then, takes place at the level of the virtual. The claim that 'there are no things' is also to be situated on this level.

Indeed, creation as a whole necessarily involves a kind of formal dualism: on the one hand, there is the process of creation, its dynamic act, and on the other, what is created, the *coagulated creativity*, the creature. Deleuze, too, borrowing from Bergson in this regard, likewise distinguishes between the virtual and the actual as two ways of being.

Creativity and the virtual

It is clear from the outset that, although the actual is not a 'lesser' state of being for Deleuze, creativity is a process that is initiated at the level of the virtual. There is, moreover (or there should be – Deleuze is not always so clear about this) a tendency of the actual to become virtual again, to 'counter-actualize', or throw off its spatial and temporal limits and regain an infinite velocity. However, actuality itself is the result of creativity, of the positive processes of incurred in the production of multiplicities:

> One only has to replace the actual terms in the movement that produces them, to bring them back to the virtuality actualized in them, in order to see that differentiation is never a negation but a creation, and that difference is never negative but essentially positive and creative. (B, 103)

The very process of actualization is thus guided by difference and creation.[3] This does not mean, however, that the virtual is an active creative instance, as opposed to being a passive, actual 'createdness'. If this were so, the virtual would be placing itself in a sort of 'transcendent' position in relation to the actual.

The transition from virtuality to actuality happens through an *immanent* differentiation of the virtual. For Deleuze, the virtual is not transcendent, even if it is *the transcendental*: it is the condition of a possibility for creation – though the transcendental is thought immanently. However, when something is divided in two, it is always difficult to achieve and maintain balance; in this case, moreover, we can ask, how can we keep the balance within being between the virtual and the actual? In practical terms, it is all too easy to let one of the two parties take the upper hand – in this case, it is easy to discern a tendency in Deleuze's writings to privilege the virtual as the source of creativity and as the plane where all processes of creation take place at an infinite speed. As Peter Hallward defends in his famous interpretation of Deleuze: 'we'll see that *purely* creative processes can only take place in a wholly virtual dimension and must operate at a literally infinite speed.'[4] It is indeed true that, for Deleuze, the process of creation initially starts at the level of the virtual: 'Virtuality exists in such a way that it actualizes itself as it dissociates itself; it must dissociate itself to actualize itself. Differentiation is the movement of a virtuality actualizing itself' (DI, 40).

The movements of counter-actualization and deterritorialization likewise indicate that, for Deleuze, creativity is to be found in the domain of the virtual (or at least it has to originate there). Counter-actualization or counter-effectuation is the process that affirms 'that part [of an event] which goes beyond [its actual] accomplishment, the immaculate part' (D, 49). It is the transition from actual to virtual: 'The event is actualized or effectuated whenever it is inserted, willy-nilly, into a state of affairs; but it is *counter-effectuated* whenever it is abstracted from states of affairs so as to isolate its concept' (WP, 159). However, the processes of actualization and counter-actualization are not just two opposite directions of the same road: 'We do not ascend and descend in this way on the same line: actualization and counter-effectuation are not two segments of the same line but rather different lines' (WP, 160). (The use of the words 'ascending' and 'descending' here, with the virtual being located in the highest regions, again, seem to suggest the privilege of the virtual.) The process of counter-actualization leads to a kind of 'purer' virtual plane, as the event that counter-actualizes 'delimits the original, disengages from it an abstract line, and keeps from the event only its contour and its splendor' (LS, 150). This kind of selection or fine-tuning of the virtual will also be effectuated through the movement of repetition. The concept of becoming-imperceptible, as explained in the previous chapter, is a good example here of Deleuze's plea for counter-actualization.

Comparable to counter-actualization is the process of deterritorialization, a concept often used by Deleuze and Guattari, which will be discussed more thoroughly in the next chapter. In short, it is the process that liberates events and things from their limits, their 'usual' territory.

We should not forget, however, that for Deleuze – and as has been pointed out already in the introduction to this chapter – the virtual is not an untouchable instance, a transcendent catalyst within the creative process. The virtual dynamic of being is influenced and changed by actualities. Consequently, the actual becomes the dimension that keeps the virtual dynamic: the virtual remains the condition of possibility, although it continuously undergoes changes due to the presence of the actual (as it is not predictable in terms of the exact virtual flow that is going to actualize and one that is not) and the corresponding counter-actualizations. It seems more fertile in fact not to see the relationship between the virtual and the actual as a duality and certainly not to see them as being opposite to each other. The virtual is more like the encompassing, omnipresent field underlying all processes of actualization that remain yet a part of the virtual. In Chapter 1, I referred to the analogy of the earth's crust (actual) and its lava (virtual), which is a helpful one perhaps as the earth's crust is yet made of lava just as the actual is yet made of the virtual.

The being intertwined and reciprocal constituting of the virtual and the actual is an idea that Deleuze has in common with the British philosopher and mathematician Alfred North Whitehead (1861–1947). Deleuze had great admiration for Whitehead's philosophy of creativity. In fact, as Keith Robinson notes, 'Whitehead's later thought functions as a central source for a good deal of what motivates Deleuze's entire philosophical project.'[5] Both Deleuze and Whitehead developed a 'metaphysics of the new', and according to James Williams, Whitehead's thought might help to articulate the reciprocal relations between the actual and the virtual in an accurate way.[6] Moreover – this is especially interesting within the context of this book – Whitehead's philosophical system lies at the base of a whole strand of thought within theology: process theology.

The introduction of Whitehead at this point will facilitate the connection of Deleuze's thoughts on creativity with those theologies of creation I seek to develop further in connection with Deleuze's work in the second part. There I will argue that Deleuze could contribute directly to a renewal of process theology, which, for its part, sometimes tends to stick within more traditional discourses as it has often tried to adapt its system to Christianity.[7] In that sense, Deleuze could effectuate a moment of liberation within process theology and consequently take this theology step further in a creative sense. Concerning the concept of God, Whitehead might in fact be closer to Deleuze than Spinoza. In Spinoza, there is no room for empirical contingency, and thus, according to Whitehead's interpretation, it is impossible for Spinoza to think real novelty.[8] Whitehead interprets Spinoza's God as an actuality (because it is the substance) who exists beyond the existence of his attributes and modes. But to be able to create novelty, God needs to be thought of as virtual.[9]

In an article on Deleuze and Whitehead, James Williams compares Deleuze's account of the virtual and the actual with Whitehead's primordial and consequent nature of God: 'God's consequent nature comes from actual creations, each one creating a new valuation and a new series of relation between eternal objects, but each novel creation comes from a creative pull in God's primordial nature.'[10] In Whitehead's philosophical system, the actual (God's consequent nature or the many) influences and even changes the virtual (God's primordial nature or the one); and while the primordial nature of God is a form of pure potentiality for Whitehead, his consequent nature is both physical and actual. The actual therefore ensures that the virtual does not become a static transcendence. Indeed, there are continuous fluxes and becomings between the two ways of being.[11] 'It is as true to say that God creates the World, as that the World creates God,'[12] Whitehead concludes. Williams names this a 'creative circle':

This creative circle moving from abstract eternal realm through a creative transformation in the actual and back to a now transformed virtual realm is akin to Deleuze's circle of destiny and his rejection of fatalism (LS, 149), where Ideas or sense move through surface or intensity to an actual realm, where a counter-actualisation reworks the form and power of the virtual, sending it back to return again as new creativity. (LS, 151)[13]

Avoiding the connection of the virtual with transcendence and the actual with immanence, Deleuze describes immanence (borrowing from Nicholas of Cusa and Giordano Bruno) as 'a coexistence of two movements – *complication* and *explication*, where God "complicates each thing" while "each thing explicates" God' (TRM, 266). The whole process of creation, therefore, consists of these two movements between the virtual and the actual.

Whitehead, for his part, would seem to connect the consequent nature of God with the movement of complication, whereas the primordial nature of God is the movement of explication. Deleuze formulates this as follows: 'The multiple is in the one which complicates it, as much as the one is in the multiple which explicates it' (TRM, 266). In other words, God is needed to explain 'the puzzling fact that there is an actual course of events which is itself a limited fact, in that metaphysically speaking it might have been otherwise'.[14] According to Steven Shaviro, Whitehead uses the notion of God to connect the virtual with the actual and to assure transition and communication between the two dimensions. If everything would be virtual 'there would be nothing but flows, nothing but rhizomes, nothing but connections and cuts. Everything would flow, and every flow would intersect with many other flows.'[15] We do not, however, live in a world that could be conceived as a 'pure rhizome' – if we would constantly live between flows and rhizomes, nothing would ever actualize, nothing would ever *happen*. That is why Whitehead in a certain sense needs the idea of God as the 'principle of concretion': this principle is necessary for anything to actualize at all. This notion is somewhat akin to Deleuze's plane of immanence or as Shaviro suggests, is aligned with Deleuze's concept of the 'Body without Organs': 'Much like the Body without Organs, God is only a quasi-cause. He does not actually create the universe: for Whitehead, creation happens in the concrescent decisions of all actual occasions, just as, for Deleuze and Guattari, creation is the productive activity of all the desiring machines.'[16] By labelling God as a quasi-cause, Shaviro safeguards the role of immanence in the process of creation. The plane of immanence, in this respect, serves as an empty plane on which creative processes can take place. Despite this apparent reality, it is not Shaviro's aim to 'identify Whitehead's God with the Body without Organs, but only to suggest that the two concepts are structurally parallel. They both respond to the same necessity: that of conceiving a non-totalizing and open "whole" in which all potentiality may be expressed. A metaphysics of process and becoming cannot do without some principle of unification, lest it drift off into atomized incoherence.'[17]

Indeed, there are also significant differences between Deleuze's plane of immanence and Whitehead's God. In *Logic of Sense*, Deleuze had already made clear that the sense of events on a plane of immanence or a chaosmos necessarily excludes the *coherence* of a divine transcendence,[18] whereas Whitehead's God is such that it brings coherence into creation through limitation. Whitehead needs divine transcendence for events to be relevant: 'Transcendent decision includes God's decision. He is the actual entity in virtue of which the *entire* multiplicity of eternal objects obtains its graded relevance to each stage of concrescence.'[19] For both philosophers, everything is interdependent and interconnected (Whitehead's coherence – Deleuze's consistency), although they apparently differ in their response to the question of *how* everything is connected. Within the disjunction, Deleuze states how the elements are connected independent of each other (in a so-called disjunctive synthesis); whereas they are connected by the transcendent 'decision' of God, according to Whitehead. The latter admits that the demand for relevance begs for such a decision to take place. As he puts it, 'Restriction is the price of value. There cannot be value without antecedent standards of value (. . .). Thus there is an antecedent limitation among values, introducing contraries.'[20] Whitehead's God can thus be understood as a limitation of possibilities.

Concerning the question of *how* all events are connected in a disjunctive synthesis, Deleuze, for his part, however, remains rather vague. He too refers to an antecedent element or a dark precursor. Yet in many ways, we are left to wonder whether this is a remnant of a transcendent transcendental, some sort of divine element re-entering his orbit. At the least, it could be interpreted as a kind of principle of unification.

> The most important difficulty, however, remains: is it really difference which relates different to different in these intensive systems? (. . .) When we speak of communication between heterogeneous systems, of coupling and resonance, does this not imply (. . .) an identity in the agent which brings about the communication? (. . .) What is this agent, this force which ensures communication? Thunderbolts explode between different intensities, but they are preceded by an invisible, imperceptible *dark precursor*, which determines their path in advance but in reverse, as though intagliated. Likewise, every system contains its dark precursor which ensures the communication of peripheral series. (DR, 145–6)

Dark precursor or not, in opposition to Whitehead, Deleuze's 'chaosmos' does not need a 'stable actuality', one that 'secures an inevitable trend towards order'.[21] Deleuze pleads for an infinite amount of different events that can be thought together in a disjunctive synthesis but will never be harmonized.[22] Moreover, he creates a strong image to describe the interrelatedness of events in a non-orderly way: the rhizome.

Rhizome

Deleuze introduces the figure of the rhizome, a botanical term, in his philosophy in order to escape what he calls the 'logic of the tree' – another, more traditional way to interconnect things, that is, a hierarchical way. Thinking rhizomatically is a condition of possibility for creativity. Similar to all processes of creativity, it originates on the virtual level, and in using the rhizome as an image, the absolute immanence of the virtual is stressed. While tree-thinking (representational thought) still operates from a logic of cause and effect and connects points that have a particular relation with each other (in space, time or as cause–effect duo), a rhizome does not consist of points but rather of *lines*. 'There are no points or positions in a rhizome, such as those found in a structure, tree, or root. There are only lines' (ATP, 9). In the case of a tree, everything emerges from one single point, a seed in the ground; a rhizome, on the contrary, neither begins nor ends in a specific place. From this angle, it is not possible to speak of any semblance of 'oneness'. A rhizome is therefore a kind of infinite horizontal network of 'lines' that cross each other, in which a line is a way of thinking, an event that develops itself or a being that is moving. When Deleuze describes the rhizome as a connection between 'semiotic chains', with the term 'semiotic' here designating the domain of signs in a broad sense (and not only linguistically understood), it becomes clear that he wants to break free from representational language by connecting semiotics to the domain of the sensual:

> A rhizome ceaselessly establishes connections between semiotic chains, organizations of power, and circumstances relative to the arts, sciences, and social struggles. A semiotic chain is like a tuber agglomerating very diverse acts, not only linguistic, but also perceptive, mimetic, gestural, and cognitive. (ATP, 8)

A good example given in order to concretize our image of the rhizome is our use of short-term memory. In *A Thousand Plateaus*, Deleuze and Guattari praise the existence of short-term memory because it does not know a past (in which it could get stuck, as in the process of psychoanalysis). The forgetting of (relations from) the past is, for them, necessary in order to be able to create something new. Short-term memory does not utilize the methods of genealogy; it does not look at things as 'coming forth from something else'; it sees things as such and apart from each other:

> Short-term memory is in no way subject to a law of contiguity or immediacy to its object (. . .). The splendor of the short-term Idea: one writes using short-term memory, and thus short-term ideas, even if one reads or rereads using long-term memory or long-term concepts. Short-term memory includes forgetting as a process. (ATP, 17)

In order to be creative, one has to reconnect trees and roots to a rhizome: 'plug the tracings back into the map, connect the roots or trees back up with a rhizome' (ATP, 15). Only then will everything be reconnected in an immanent way; only then can everything express the force of being equally.

Creativity as repetition

It is not only the rhizome that helps us imagine the creativity of the virtual in a non-representative way, for the idea of repetition does this as well. Repetition in fact connects being and creativity with time. Deleuze is particularly inspired by Bergson here, who calls the pure, unconscious past the 'virtual'. It is a past that is not representable and that will always remain unconscious. Nevertheless, for Deleuze – in a way that is not true for Bergson – this pure past is accessible through direct experience. For example, he interprets Marcel Proust's famous Madeleine experience from the classic *In Search of Lost Time* as a direct experience of this pure past. A leap made within this specific space of memory is a leap into ontology, into being. Whereas the virtual is connected to the pure past, representation belongs to the category of the present. 'The past is pure ontology; pure recollection has only ontological significance' (B, 56). It is clear from this that the virtual is real without being actual.

The virtual is an idea, even though it has no mental character (for it is not representable): it is a power that is immanently working within this life.[23] Then how can the virtual be valued, if it cannot be thought consciously? Here, the idea of repetition provides us with some help: events that are strong enough will always return; they will indeed repeat themselves. In this way, the virtual is 'preserved'. What is preserved, what is repeated, is not an actual being or an event; it is only a part of this event. The repetition is a repetition of difference – of a power that is irreplaceable.

In the famous 'Goldberg Variations' of J.S. Bach, for example, lies an intrinsic power for repetition. The theme is never repeated exactly, for Bach tries to capture the *power* of the theme in each variation. What is stressed is the aspect of *productivity* instead of conservation. Because of this, although the virtual is linked to the past, repetition is essentially aimed towards the *future*: it detaches from its origin, and if it is powerful enough, it will make endless beginnings, that is, it returns forever. Here, we recognize perhaps something of Nietzsche's 'Eternal Return'. What returns is not the Truth or the Essence of the event: it is that which is *powerful enough*. Thinking is living insofar as it is productive, creative and renewing.[24] The possibilities for a new conception of (theological) tradition as repetition, if viewed from this perspective, are certainly exciting, for if tradition becomes repetition, not in a conservative, but in a productive sense, theology could be reconnected to life with a renewed significance. (I will develop this thought in part two of this chapter.)

Obviously, for Deleuze, repetition does not indicate that the same thing returns again and again. In the introduction to *Difference and Repetition*, Deleuze describes two ways of thinking repetition: 'real' repetition, understood as Deleuze feels it has to be, and 'generality' or the order of resemblance and equivalence, which is something totally different. 'Repetition and resemblance are different in kind – extremely so' (DR, 1). Real repetitions 'do not add a second and a third time to the first, but carry the first time to the "nth" power (. . .) as Péguy says, it is not Federation Day which commemorates or represents the fall of the Bastille, but the fall of the Bastille which celebrates and repeats in advance all the Federation Days' (DR, 2). Translated into Christian theological terms, we might say: it is not the Eucharist which commemorates and represents the event of Christ but the event of Jesus Christ's life, death and resurrection, which celebrates and repeats in advance all Eucharists!

The difference between the two formulations has important and lasting consequences: when understood in a Deleuzian sense, what is repeated in the Eucharist is the *power* of Jesus Christ's life. It transcends the particular laws and prescriptions which the church holds on to concerning the Eucharist: in Catholicism, for example, the Eucharist should be celebrated only by an ordained, male priest, and the words that are pronounced during the process of this sacrament, should always literally be the same. Contrary to these formulations, Deleuze would appear to bring the Eucharist back to what it really is: a miracle.

> If repetition is possible, it is due to miracle rather than to law. It is against the law: against the similar form and the equivalent content of law. If repetition can be found, even in nature, it is in

the name of a power which affirms itself against the law, which works underneath laws, perhaps superior to laws. If repetition exists, it expresses at once a singularity opposed to the general, a *universality opposed to the particular*, a distinctive opposed to the ordinary, an instantaneity opposed to variation and an eternity opposed to permanence. In every respect, repetition is a transgression. It puts law into question, it denounces its nominal or general character in favour of a more profound and more artistic reality. (DR, 3, my emphasis)

The power of an event that returns cannot be grasped within representational thinking. The language in which one speaks about this power must necessarily be lyrical, not scientific, Deleuze remarks, because in lyrical language, 'every term is irreplaceable and can only be repeated' (DR, 2). Applied to poetry – though this also counts for sacramental language, or the language of a prayer for that matter, 'it is not by chance that a poem must be learned by heart. The head is the organ of exchange, but the heart is the amorous organ of repetition' (DR, 2).

From a classical Christian perspective, one might now perhaps object and respond that, in the Eucharist, and in the whole of the Christian tradition, what is repeated is not merely an impersonal power but the power of one particular man – of Jesus Christ. Again, we must recall that for Deleuze, repetition has nothing to do with the generality of a vague power. In the process of a repetition, the universal and the singular are reunited, 'which dethrones every general law; dissolves the mediations and annihilates the particulars subjected to the law' (DR, 8). By interpreting the Christian tradition as the repetition of (the event of) Jesus Christ, the singularity, uniqueness and the universal significance of his life, are expressed. Through the Eucharist, we could experience (not represent!) the power of the life of Christ. What is repeated, then, is irreplaceable.

Of course, for Deleuze, Christ is not the only event that can be repeated. Deleuze is moreover certainly not a Christian theologian. Any event that is forceful enough, is worthy of being repeated. The subject of the repetition is *difference* – a non-representable, positive force: 'It is a question of knowing why repetition cannot be explained by the form of identity in concepts or representations; in what sense it demands a superior "positive" principle' (DR, 22). Yet Christianity has an important lesson to learn here: through his account of repetition, Deleuze offers religion a new approach to the tension between universality and particularity that touches the very core of what it means to belong to a tradition. It is our task to 'become worthy of the event' (LS, 149) so that the event is able to repeat itself infinitely, not always in the same form but always recognizable as a virtual force that is directed towards the future because it has been able to detach itself from its origins. Only then can repetition equal creativity.

Another significant characteristic of repetition in the sense that Deleuze uses it is that it is selective. It is never the event as a whole that returns. The process of repetition selects only the positive force of difference. When he explains this, Deleuze refers once more to Nietzsche's account of the Eternal Return: 'The secret of Nietzsche is *that the eternal Return is selective*. (. . .) Only affirmation comes back, only that which can be affirmed returns, only joy returns.'[25] The negative cannot return, because for Nietzsche, the negative is reactive and eventually nihilistic. The Eternal Return is being itself as understood from the perspective of affirmation and becoming.[26] It is almost logic impossibility that the negative carries a creative force within itself. Being selective is therefore not a negative process that does away with certain aspects of being; to the contrary, it is supposed to be a *liberating selection* as the process of repetition 'saves' the very force of difference.[27]

> The eternal Return should be compared with a wheel; but the movement of the wheel is cursed with a centrifugal power, which chases away all the negative from the center. Because Being affirms itself through becoming, it rejects everything that contradicts the affirmation, all forms of nihilism and reaction: bad conscience, resentment. . ., one will only experience those once.[28]

As the connection of repetition with Nietzsche's Eternal Return demonstrates, repetition is not only a concept that explains how being is creativity, it is also a highly ethical notion. As I have already mentioned, for Deleuze, living an ethical life means being worthy of the event – living in such a way that the event repeats itself, that it returns eternally. Nietzsche makes this concrete by asking how we need to live in order to justify the return of even the most painful event? This question could certainly allow us to make a more 'Paulist' interpretation of the meaning of Jesus Christ's life, in which the crucifixion becomes a positive power that is worthy to be repeated (we all die with Christ!) – not the crucifixion itself, but the power of it. In this sense, the *resurrection* could already be interpreted as the *repetition of Jesus' death*: it repeats the positive power of the event of Jesus' death, namely, the taking away of our sins and affirming that life conquers death. Through this repetition, all the negative is expelled from the event.

As such, Deleuze's account of creativity as repetition could renew the Christian idea of tradition and the interpretation of Jesus' life and suffering. What is important to remember is that repetition for Deleuze is a 'fundamental category of a philosophy of the *future*' (DR, 6, my emphasis). Being the expression of a force directed towards the future, repetition is not about those particularities that are repeated and represented, but about a *reproduction* that expresses something new (because it is a reproduction of difference, not of identity). It is like the reproduction of a movie that tries to capture the force of the first version but can allow itself to deviate from the 'original' version. Repetition is the affirmation of the new, and in that sense, it is always a 'beginning again'. Despite this fact, however, the beginning is not the origin! As we will see in what follows, these insights have great repercussions for a theology of creation.

Theologies of creation – creative theologies

In theological terms, creation refers to God's creation of the world, understood as an exclusively divine activity, a creation out of nothing – *creatio ex nihilo*. By indicating that there was nothing before God undertook the action to create heaven, earth and all the rest, believers want to stress God's uniqueness and transcendence. *Creatio ex nihilo* can be interpreted as a symbol of our absolute dependence on God: only God can make the transition from non-being to being. Moreover, creation happened as a result of God's initiative; it was God's free will, the result of God's abundant love. This stands of course in sharp contrast with Deleuze's account of creation out of necessity: one creates because it is the necessary step towards solving a problem, to liberate the force of difference. 'There has to be a necessity, in philosophy and elsewhere; otherwise there is nothing. A creator is not a preacher working for the fun of it. A creator only does what he or she absolutely needs to do' (TRM, 318). Moreover, in Christian theology, creation is ethically qualified as intrinsically good. It is an answer to the question: why is there anything at all rather than nothing? The answer is because God's love was so great that God, in all generosity, created the world and gave us life. The doctrine of creation expresses the belief that God is the ultimate source, ground and goal of all things visible and invisible.[29] Human beings occupy a special place within God's creation: they are the 'shepherds' of the rest of creation.

There is indeed a clear hierarchy within creation. Taking Darwin's theory of evolution into account, it is believed that God has created the world in such a way that there is an evolution towards intelligent life, that is, that human beings are the 'top' of the pyramid. This is called the 'anthropic principle', of which God is said to be the transcendental ground. However, another theological 'answer' to the demands of natural science concerning creation that is perhaps more interesting in this context, is that of *creatio continua*. Such a notion is a theological idea that has always remained marginal but has finally been accepted next to (and subordinate to) the doctrine of creation out of nothing as a kind of completion of that theory. The emphasis now lies on novelty and preserving care. Continuous creation is a creation of 'order out of chaos,' an idea that is more akin to scientific research.[30] The idea of a creation 'out of chaos' has also been picked up by process theologians, although they confirmed a creation out of chaos based on scientific motivations and without connecting it to a biblical tradition.

It is clear, however, that in the context of an encounter with Deleuze, the idea of continuous creation should receive more attention. From a Deleuzian perspective, it is also possible to formulate a critique of the doctrine of creation out of nothing. What is at stake here is not only a question of an origin or a beginning but also of an *ethical* nature: the idea of *creatio ex nihilo* installs God as a transcendent, supernatural instance above the natural world that does not have to deal with any 'other'. Chaos is systematically erased or ignored within this world view. According to the American theologian Catherine Keller, who seeks to reconnect a creation out of chaos with the Biblical tradition, chaos is traditionally associated with 'formless monsters, maternal hysteria, pagan temptation, dark hoards, caves of terror, contaminating hybrids, miscegenation and sexual confusion'.[31] In her book *The Face of the Deep: A Theology of Becoming*, Keller pleads for a theology of creation as a 'beginning' (a beginning which, according to literary theorist and postcolonial thinker Edward Said, is always relative, contested and historical)[32] and not as an absolute 'origin'. A beginning is not a linear concept. Throughout her book, in fact, Keller demonstrates this biblically, narratively and hermeneutically. Through this exercise, another, marginalized side of the tradition is unveiled. Said formulates this accurately in his work 'Beginnings' where he states: 'Whereas an origin *centrally* dominates what derives from it, the beginning (. . .) encourages nonlinear development, a logic giving rise to the sort of multileveled coherence of dispersion.'[33] From this beginning, Keller wishes to develop a new theology of creation, a constructive theology of the deep.[34] She connects this theology of creation with process thought, feminist theory, environmental and postcolonial issues.

Instead of elaborating extensively on the affinities between Deleuze and process theology, I would like to draw attention to specific interesting undercurrents in and beyond process theology that also try to break open the still very classical theological framework of process theology. Keller, for example, develops a *constructive* theology of 'becoming' based on a creation out of chaos that is in line with Deleuze's account of creativity. Relational theologies, furthermore, also provide more positive theologies. They benefit from the concept of the rhizome in order to further develop the non-hierarchical and non-representational account of relationality that is the basis of those theologies. Finally, I will again elaborate on the idea of thinking tradition as repetition in the Deleuzian sense because it is my belief that by combining those two concepts, tradition can again become creative.

One of the strongest points of Deleuze's thinking comes to the fore in his theory of creativity: he combines, in a very non-postmodern manner, a form of 'total critique' with a positive, constructive theory. The notion of 'total critique' here is borrowed from Nietzsche, for whom it concerned a negation that is not a form of dialectics: there is no third term possible. 'Deleuze's total critique [of a preconstituted order of being] involves a destruction so absolute that it becomes necessary to question what makes reality possible,'[35] or so Michael Hardt contends. Only such a radical negation makes creation both possible and necessary. Nowadays, a theology that is confronted with postmodern philosophy often ends up being little more than a negative theology. Deleuze provides a theology that wishes to engage with philosophical theories with a metaphysics that allows for a positive, constructive theology that remains at the same time very critical towards a modern logic of representation.

Creation out of chaos and the virtuality of God

Keller's critique of a concept of creation from nothing is very much akin to Deleuze's critique of representation. Moreover, Keller also points towards the political consequences of a theology that adheres to a notion of creation from nothing. This is not merely a theoretical–doctrinal quarrel. The difference between a creation from nothing and a creation out of chaos affects the core of our being and our place in the world. Keller, for her part, accuses the Christian anthropology that comes forth from a *creatio ex nihilo* as being in league with modern forms of colonialism. The human race, Western civilization in particular, has shown a tendency to dominate the rest of creation, to order the universe on its terms, based on a consciousness of a privileged place within creation. The way that an omnipotent God created the world, namely, by creating order out of nothing, by pushing away anything that looks like chaos or darkness, inspired the privileged race, so the narrative goes, to hold on to this dynamic of creating order by means of constructing hierarchies, and disregarding 'anything or anyone else', as if there were nothing and no one before its intervention.

It is only in the late second century that the patriarchal idea of a creation from nothing was developed. Augustine fully articulated the doctrine only in the fourth century, the formal point when Chaos was finally conquered.

> The idea of a creation from nothing rather than a formation from formlessness only gradually ensconced itself in Christian common sense. Along with it settled the dogmas of omnipotence: not just of the biblical lord of great if somewhat unpredictable power, but an immutable, unilateral All-Power clothed in the attributes of a single male Person (or two; or . . .). Is it then the orthodox postulate, rather than the universe, which got produced from nothing?[36]

If the idea of a creation from nothing has been historically constructed by patriarchal theologians, what and where are the remnants of the chaos that was believed in before this doctrinal intervention? Furthermore, how do these elements alter our idea of creation?

In *The Face of the Deep*, Keller undertakes a journey past Jewish and old Christian traditions (utilizing mainly the Bible and Jewish commentaries) in order to demonstrate how chaos was still present in the belief of many people and how it was suppressed by a few dominant thinkers throughout time. It goes without saying that our view of creation within Christianity would radically change if we would allow chaos to re-enter.

This is precisely Keller's thought experiment. Her book is one great plea to convince us of the obviousness of allowing chaos to thrive within theology: 'For a theology of becoming, it is precisely the dichotomy of "making" and "letting be" that Genesis precludes. How else does Elohim *make* – but *by* letting be: "And God said: *let* there be. . ."?'[37] Moreover, apart from the fact that chaos has always been a (hidden) part of our tradition of a theology of creation, it opens up a theology of creation towards the future. 'The question is whether the theology of creation keeps the future wide and *opening*.'[38] A theology of creation should be concerned with the creation of *vital space* – to use a concept of the Brazilian liberation theologian Vitor Westhelle.[39] In this sense, creation becomes a political matter.

In the tradition of political and liberation theologies, this is new as these theologies were never really engaged by a theology of creation: it seemed of secondary importance, too abstract for the precarious contexts they sometimes worked within. Within the Christian tradition, they felt more connected with biblical accounts of the Exodus and the cross. 'Creation discourse seems to be so detached from the dramatic demands of immediate life that to dwell on it would mean to be oblivious to more demanding and life-threatening questions.'[40] Moreover, creation was automatically associated with 'order' (and the expulsion of chaos). 'Order' was not liberation theology's most favoured concept, mainly because it was considered to be 'most often an ideological disguise for domination, repression, and persecution. (. . .) What lacks order, lacks goodness. Lack of order is evil. Whatever is anomalous and conflictive must be integrated into a well-ordered center or be annihilated. By such criteria people have been exiled and are homeless.'[41] This association in itself, however, grants creation theology a political core.

Whitney Bauman too connects the concept of *creatio ex nihilo* with politics. According to him, this projecting of an ultimate origin is directly linked to the colonial idea of the *terra nullius*: many areas where colonialists arrived were assumed to belong to no one and then became automatically owned by the 'conqueror,' thereby denying the presence of other peoples and traditions, while destroying them.

> The doctrine of *ex nihilo* serves to sever Christian beginnings from (other) Ancient Near Eastern traditions, as if "other" histories could be encompassed by the Christian One, and to project the One Christian history onto all others, thereby incorporating, ignoring, or erasing other peoples' histories. In this way, *ex nihilo* functions to deny the presence of other's truth-claims on reality in a similar way that *terra nullius* functions to deny the presence of colonized others some 1,400 years later.[42]

Underneath the logic of the creation from nothing, Keller traces another suppressed tradition of creation in the Bible, a creation out of the depths of chaos, the 'tehom' as the Hebrew Bible formulates it in the second verse of Genesis 1: 'Now the earth was formless and empty, darkness was over the surface of the deep [*tehom*]. . . .' Depth is not interpreted in a vertical way, then, but horizontally, as a width, or as a 'chaos from which difference unfolds a cosmos. Thus the multidimensional surfaces of heaven-and-earth – its water, earth and atmosphere, its multiple species and societies – disseminate the deep.'[43] Depth is interpreted here in a very Deleuzian sense, as indistinguishable from difference, a 'matrix of the unequal and the different' (DR, 335). Indeed, Keller herself admits the fertility of Deleuze's account of 'depth' in this context: 'Deleuze especially will facilitate the articulation of a tehomic relation of "chaos" to "depth".'[44] Inspired by Deleuze, for whom meaning can only be an effect on the surface of the plane of immanence, Keller interprets 'depth' as the virtual:

> The distinctions of above/below, figure/ground, which define the conventional meaning of 'depth', for him [Deleuze] 'flow from a "deeper" instance – depth itself, which is not an extension but a pure implex'. In other words depth is not 'a dimension' but the dimensionality out of which the spatiotemporal dimensions unfold. To unfold is to 'explicate'.[45]

Despite this, however, Deleuze is not the only thinker who helps Keller in articulating the importance of the *tehom* as the beginning of creation. *Tehom* is linked to a whole series of concepts used by both Derrida and Deleuze that stem from older philosophers and have one thing in common: they all express a non-representable condition of possibility for actualities and events:

> That depth of beginning cross-cuts in theory the 'chaotic variability' of a proliferating matrix of tehomic icons: *différance*, creativity, trace, khora, infinity, *complicatio* [sic], multiplicity, the heterogeneous dimension. As *dimensionality* rather than as a dimension, the depth enfolds an infinity of virtual finitudes: the creations, the creatures. They *are* not chaos, but the organized explications of its dimensions. 'Art is not chaos but a composition of chaos,' say Deleuze and Guattari, so that it constitutes 'a chaosmos, a composed chaos – neither foreseen nor preconceived' (WP, 204). We may readily imagine Elohim's creativity as closer to art than to science.[46]

Keller thus interprets *tehom* as the virtual, the condition of possibility for creativity, the plane of immanence on which the process of creation takes place: 'Might tehom henceforth suggest the chaoid (. . .) multidimensionality of a bottomless deep: the matrix in which creation *becomes*?'[47]

But what then is the relation of God to this *tehom*? From the perspective of process theology, we should identify *tehom*, as the virtual, with the primordial nature of God; it is the ultimate ground and source of our experience that is, for Whitehead, a metaphysically (and rationally) necessary ground utilized in order to think creativity and to account for the complexity of reality. The primordial nature of God, however, does not provide us with a complete image of God – it has to be complemented with the consequent nature of God. Again, Keller finds traces of this primordial nature of God in the Bible. In Hebrew, the most ancient word for God used is in fact the plural word 'Elohim': Gods. Traditionally, the plural form of the word was explained by referring to the power and plenitude of God, although Keller proposes to take the 'residual multiplicity with theological seriousness,'[48] just as some Jewish Rabbis did when they made reference to angels. Keller refers to another scholar, Lynn Bechtel, to describe how the multiple is divinized: 'In further exegetical attestation of this elemental Elohimic multiple, Lynn Bechtel translates "Elohim" as "differential unity," appropriate to a "group orientation" where individuality comes only embedded in collectivity and nature. (. . .) Creation takes place *within* a fluid interdimensionality.'[49]

Having uncovered the hidden tradition of creation out of chaos and having connected the chaos with the virtual nature of being/God, an important question arises: how can we think creativity as the emergence of the *new* when it is not created 'from nothing'? Two concepts of Deleuze will helps us to answer this question: the figure of the 'fold' on the virtual level, and the 'event' that is actual (insofar as virtual and actual can be considered separately – all actualities are part of the fold, and, in their actuality, they share a virtual core[50]). A third concept related to this question, repetition, will be treated more explicitly later in this chapter.

Other than in Alain Baidou's philosophy of event, where the event requires freedom from any context or attachment, the Deleuzian event emerges out of the fold of the universe. Indeed, the virtual is imagined as a fold, it presents an 'origami universe'. Both Catherine Keller and Keith Robinson translate the fold as Whitehead's concept of 'prehension' – the sensible condition for experience: 'the fold, precisely translated as prehension, suggests connec-tivity, drapes waves, intertwinings.'[51] The event then, bursts out of the fold, intensifies 'novelty in explosion'.[52] To the extent that the event contracts time and interrupts the linear conception of time, does it not 'mimic a long tradition of explosive Christian eschatology?'[53] The event of Christ, for example, was always believed to break through the circles of the surrounding 'heathen' conceptions of time.

If we are to repeat the Christ-event with the same intensity as it had some 2000 years ago, we have to adopt another conception of 'the new' that is neither a material nor a transcendent one. The God of the creation of nothing created everything 'from nothing', in the material sense and thereby consolidated a sovereign sense of transcendence over the material. Deleuze, however, has taught us to think not in terms of 'objects' but in terms of 'relations' and the dynamics of intensity. What is new in an event are precisely the *connections* that are made. Creation is thus not a matter of emanation, where the act of creation comes forth from one instance – it is an immanent process of contractions in time. The fold, or the prehension, or the chaos, is the (real) condition for a creative event to take place:

> Prehension [as condition for the event of the new] is a non-cognitive 'feeling' that guides how the occasion shapes itself from the data of the past and the potentialities of the future. Prehension is an 'intermediary', a purely immanent potential power, a relation of difference with itself, of pure 'affection' before any division into form and matter. Prehension, for Deleuze, is a passage or folding 'between' states, a movement of pure experience or perception that increases or decreases its potential through interaction and communication with those states.[54]

The result of seeing events as contractions of time, creating new connections within the folds of the universe, is an immanent, pantheist 'chaosmos' in which everything is an expression of divine creativity:

> What we call wheat is a contraction of the earth and humidity, and this contraction is both a contemplation and the auto satisfaction of that contemplation. By its existence alone, the lily of the flied sings the glory of the heavens the goddesses and gods – in other words, the elements that it contemplates in contracting. (DR, 96)

In elaborating upon Keller's theology of creation, I have tried to provide an example of what a theology of creation might look like when one starts from the Deleuzian account of creation. Such a theology, Keller has demonstrated, does not even have to be invented; there is much within the Christian tradition that hints towards what has been described as a Deleuzian interpretation of creativity. Visualized, we should try to imagine this new theology of creation as a rhizome rather than as a tree or another 'hierarchical' image that allows for a top–down representation of creation. The image of the rhizome implies an interconnectedness of all creatures. This relational account of creation have been stressed by the so-called relational theologies. And how might the figure of the rhizome help these theologies to articulate their account of relation more accurately, or how would the intrusion of the rhizome change the idea they have of relationality?

Rhizomes of interrelatedness

Creativity, as an ongoing process, takes place on a horizontal level. From a theological perspective, bringing the horizontal concept of the rhizome into theology means taking away the teleology from within theology – something that is quite a fundamental problem. If this were done, there would be no goal affixed anymore to creation. Where a classical account of creation theology includes the aim of all creatures to 'climb up' to their originator God again, this ascending movement of the creatures completely disappears in a theology of creation formulated from a Deleuzian perspective. Due to his metaphysics of univocity, one is already God. There is a univocal relation between creatures (beings) and creator (being). If there is some sort of aim within a rhizomatic theology, it would be the expansion of the rhizomatic network, making more connections – as many as possible – like the rampant growth of weeds. Then God is expressed (as a dynamic, creative force) in infinitely different ways, through an uncountable quantity of connections, though it is still God.

Thinking creation as a rhizome obviously also means that there is no hierarchy anymore in creation. Humans are no longer 'shepherds' over the rest of creation; they cannot relate themselves to the rest of creation as 'objects' anymore, as if there were a gap between human beings and the rest of creation, one that places humans in a dominant position over against the rest of creation – for even if this position is filled in with loving, responsible care, the structure remains one of hierarchy. It is not difficult to discern the logic of representation at work here. The world is objectified and represented by humanity as an object outside of it. In this way, human will and law are imposed upon the rest of creation. In contrast to this traditional account of the relationship between creatures, a rhizome 'simply grows' in all directions, though it remains a horizontal plane. The relation between human beings and other creatures then is one of equality; in no way, could one or both parties transcend the other.

As a consequence, relational theologies obviously do not solely focus on the relationship between human beings and God. Anthropocentrism is the greatest enemy of this theology; relational theologies give 'agency to all living things and the cosmos itself'.[55] Relational theologies are inherently creative, for they are *formed in the interactions.*[56] Relational theologies differ from the mainstream tradition most of all in their method, which is based on experience. In this respect, they relate to Deleuze's method of 'pure empiricism'. As Keller puts it, 'the Deleuzian relationality seems to surface mainly in relations or rhizomes, within the nonhuman, the 'subpersonal', hence the molecular – kin to Leibniz's closed monads and Whitehead's open organisms.'[57]

Deleuze's empiricism takes into account the experiences, not only of women and men but also of the whole cosmos, so that even the smallest particle has its place in the rhizome of interrelatedness. In fact, through this severe form of empiricism, the subject as such completely disappears – we appear to be an assemblage of an infinite amount of particles and dynamics: 'we speak of our "self" only in virtue of these thousands of little witnesses which contemplate within us . . .' (DR, 96). Although it seems obvious to state that all theology is relational, in practice this does not always seem to be the case. The very methods of relational theologies tend to break open traditional accounts of creation and the relation of creatures with the divine, for in a relational theology, God exists *only* in relations and, as a consequence, God exists only in God's creation. The following citation stresses the direction towards the future of relational theologies as well as their creative potential:

> The lived experience of women, men and the cosmos becomes the stuff of ever-emerging and changing forms of theological reflection. Fixed ends and ultimate truths so easy to declare in the light of the Word becoming flesh are transformed in the crucible of the flesh becoming word – an ever-changing word, as the realities of life unfold and spiral. Such relationality questions many of the old traditional certainties and opens up a future of endless possibility, glorious and mundane, filled with the abundance of life spoken of in the Gospels or crushed and broken by the carelessness of human creatures.[58]

However, one question still haunts us in discerning the connection of the rhizome with relational theology: what exactly does 'relation' mean? Are Deleuze and relational theologies talking about the same kind of relation? What about, for example, Deleuze's understanding of 'the other' as mere context (see Chapter 2), as something that distracts you from performing your spiritual task in this world? What about his idea of the 'disjunctive synthesis' – in which all different entities exist independently from one another and are only connected through their source, that is, being? I suggest reading this disjunctive synthesis positively, as a relatedness of beings *within* being that at the same time respects their differences – the difference in power, velocity and intensity (other, representational differences do not exist in Deleuze's univocal universe).

This understanding of the relational could help broaden the scope of relational theologies that otherwise often remain 'contextual', that is, as particular theologies only. Deleuze teaches us to connect beyond contexts, though at a 'molecular' level. As such, it is not the visible differences and similarities between people and things that matter but the invisible lines of convergence (crossroads, becomings and events!) and divergence in intensity, velocity and power that express our relation with the divine. Processes of becoming, for example, are rhizomes formed at the molecular level. Becoming-animal, for Deleuze and Guattari, does not mean that we start to resemble a certain animal but that we 'access' or 'enter' an animal at a molecular level. It is about 'tuning into' the intensity of the animal, and there a rhizome is formed between humans and animals.[59]

Relational theology already points towards the importance of the (molecular) community – a theme I will discuss in the next chapter. Spirituality is therefore not private and certainly not a 'personal' affair: it is a matter of making new connections, of getting rid of the personal. It is about 'transcending human skin and human identity.'[60]

The figure of the rhizome supports the idea of a creation out of chaos, and relational theologies too share in this perspective on creation. Relationality is always an immanent affair and an ethical one – it is opposed to a dialectical (Hegel) or an analogical relation (Aquinas).[61]

Tradition as repetition

Another way of thinking the process of creativity as the production of something new formed out of chaos is through the concept of repetition. As seen above, I have already pointed out how the repetition of an event of the 'pure past' (that is not representable) is not the recapturing of an old event in history but is directed towards the future. In the process of repetition, the event has detached itself from its origins and makes a new beginning. Repetition becomes the expression of something new – and thereby it becomes inherently creative – because it is the repetition of difference, not of identity. An event that is repeated in no way resembles the 'original' event to which it refers. The reference only concerns the *power* of the original event, the intensity that is the creative power through which the event is repeated.

If I define the Christian tradition as the repetition of the Christ-event, how does that affect our understanding of tradition? First of all, tradition becomes connected with creativity and the new. This seems to be a contradiction given the fact that the Christ-event might not be repeatable or bring forth something new because it is an event that is already fully accomplished: in Christ, God has revealed Godself definitely, once and for all. What can be revealed through repetition afterwards is nothing but a pale blueprint of that single event. But what if we let Deleuze challenge the theological conception of the definitive revelation of God in Christ? Then what is revealed through Christ is not so much the fact of *who God is* but the *power God has* – the *intensity of God's life*. In this respect, every event that takes place within the Christian tradition and that is meant to repeat the Christ-event is able to create what is forever new.

Second, understanding tradition as repetition in the Deleuzian sense radically changes our idea of what tradition is. Throughout history, there has always been a tension concerning the core of the tradition: does tradition have a permanent core that is wrapped up differently in every time and place, or is the 'wrapping', the cultural and historical package that we hand over to the next generation, the only thing there really is and is it therefore impossible to speak about an absolute, universal and transcendent core? Formulating an answer to this problem in a Deleuzian sense, I would say that there cannot be a representable core of tradition, and it is definitely not to be repeated. However, tradition might be more than just a hollow box, a collection of externalities that are being adapted to 'the signs of the time' every now and then. The 'core' of the Christian tradition would be the power of the Christ-event. This core is not representable, neither is it something fixed: it is an *invisible dynamic* that is immanent to all external appearances of tradition.

The belief that God has revealed Godself in an ultimate way in Christ can be 'translated' into Deleuzian terms as the belief that God's power at the moment of the Christ-event was at its summit. The Christ-event is far from finished with the life and death of Jesus Christ. On the contrary, the Christ-event is worthy of being repeated because it expressed such great power. Therefore, it is even possible to create something new through the repetition of this event, on the basis of its power that is repeated. The condition for this to happen is the detachment of the Christ-event from its origin, namely the life of Jesus. Detaching the event from its origins means to counter-actualize it, to preserve its virtual power and repeat this in, for example, an act of charity or the sacraments. Repetition could thus become a new *beginning*, as I explained above in referring to Catherine Keller's theology of becoming.

Finally, the consequences of a Deleuzian interpretation of tradition seem far-reaching from the outside: there is not one doctrine, not one ritual or other content of the tradition that is absolute or universal. The only thing universal about tradition is its invisible 'motor', the power by which it is repeated and re-invented. But the actual forms through which this power can express itself are in principle infinite (and, in practice, will depend upon the community within which these forms are actualized). The tradition can no longer hold on to its 'essences', as is the case with one of the reproaches Deleuze makes towards theology.[62] Continuity is no longer a requirement of a given tradition. Tradition as the re-presentation of a past event is thus replaced by tradition as creation, as reproduction. The subject of tradition is no longer reference to a historical person but to an (invisible) power this person expressed in their life. Tradition no longer has a visible identity. Instead, it expresses the differentiating power of God, like Origen's *Logos*, a topology that maps out the soul's transformative becoming-divine.[63]

A theology of creation thus becomes a creative theology. God is no longer the Creator; God is infinite creativity. Each act of creation is a new beginning, not an absolute origin, and Christian theology becomes a repetition of the power of the Christ-event, directed not at the past but towards the future. As a consequence, and bearing in mind the rhizomatic character of creativity, theology and Christian tradition will express itself in relation to the questions of the future. It is impossible to detach tradition from the rest of society, as if it would be a transcendent or abstract creative bubble. Tradition is faithful to an event in the past, but this is a 'pure past' that is not accessible through memories or representations.

Deleuze's understanding of repetition therefore enables us to articulate tradition as a *process of liberation* in order to see how the Christian tradition offers us room for new expressions of the encounter with God's power. Moreover, the figure of the rhizome implies that tradition is a matter of communities – it can never be created by one individual being; it is always created in an encounter that enlarges the rhizome and that creates new forms within it.

4

Ethical life

*Ethics is not the corollary of the vision of God,
it is that very vision* (Levinas, Difficult Freedom, 17).

This final chapter represents the culmination of my argument for the relevance of Deleuze to theology – especially in the areas of ethics and politics. What is particularly interesting for theology in general is the tight connection Deleuze maintains between ethics and metaphysics, a connection that results in an activist spirituality akin to theology's drive: it is about a *world view* that is *connected to a vision*, a vision that provokes spiritual and ethical action in those who believe in it.

In addition to this focus on Deleuze's uniquely relevant approach to ethics and politics, the work of Spinoza plays an implicit but important role in this chapter. After all, his ethics refer directly to actions. For Spinoza, the task – the imperative – of an ethical human being is to maximize his or her potential to act (EP, 259ff). Spinoza's shift from morality to ethics is crucial for Deleuze as well as for the encounter with theology, which I try to stage here. By engaging the two philosophers in this way, I hope to mitigate the apparent 'lack of morality' and teleology in Deleuze, which could repel theologians from engaging with his thought. Indeed, Deleuze strongly opposes any form of morality or moral laws, describing them in Spinozist terms as an 'enterprise of domination of the passions by consciousness' (PP, 18). Such moral laws are all the more problematic for Deleuze because, as he explains, the nature of consciousness is to take itself as first cause and to invoke a God where it can no longer imagine itself as the first cause (PP, 20). Such a logic of transcendence can no longer have any place in an immanentist world view. Spinoza offers the model of the body as an antidote to this logic, 'showing that the body surpasses the knowledge that we have of it, *and that thought likewise surpasses the consciousness that we have of it*' (PP, 18). Thus, it becomes necessary to replace moral laws that are rooted in consciousness with ethics which, instead, originate in the unconscious – in what will later be called *desire*. 'Ethics, which is to say, a typology of immanent modes of existence, replaces Morality, which always refers existence to transcendent values. Morality is the judgment of God, the *system of judgment*. But Ethics overthrows the system of judgment. The opposition of values (Good-Evil) is supplanted by the qualitative difference of modes of existence (good-bad)' (PP, 23).

Spinoza thus enables Deleuze to give his metaphysics of univocity and immanence a practical turn. And that is exactly what Deleuze was looking for, since for him, the problem of transcendence is not at all an abstract but a highly political matter. In this sense, Deleuze can be appropriately called a Marxist: his goal was not simply to understand reality, but to change it.[1]

I will present Deleuze's philosophy in this chapter as a political project – one that is predicated on the necessity of activism or praxis. Deleuze's most explicit analyses of capitalism and psychoanalysis were only made during a period of intense collaboration with the Félix Guattari (mostly in *Anti-Oedipus*), but it is clear that from the outset of his philosophical 'career', Deleuze interpreted his metaphysics as a practical matter, as a way of life. His understanding of ontology is, in other words, directly political. This is an approach that might seem unusual in today's philosophical academic world, but from a theological perspective, it is almost natural. From a theological standpoint, every world view is connected to a vision and, as a consequence, to a certain way of life. I would not hesitate to call every serious theology a political theology – or at least to assert that every serious theology should be political.

Deleuze's world view is not only political, it is – through its political engagement – liberating in its very core; his is a *politics of liberation*. Philosophical and political analyses are used to develop a vision of a life, which is liberated from the existing order and to effectuate a movement of active liberation from that order's hold. But also positively, this is a project of liberation: freedom – the free movement of powers and intensities – is the goal of liberation. As a force, it reaches beyond the individual. With Paul Patton, this kind of liberation could be called 'critical freedom':

> Critical freedom differs from the standard liberal concepts of positive and negative freedom by its focus upon the conditions of change or transformation in the subject, and by its indifference to the individual or collective nature of the subject. (. . .) It is the freedom to transgress the limits of what one is presently capable of being or doing, rather than just the freedom to be or do those things.[2]

This double dynamic of liberation is also constitutive of what is called 'liberation theology'. In practice, it is of course impossible to speak about one liberation theology, but despite the fragmented field of liberation theologies in the twenty-first century, they do hold several characteristics in common. Liberation theologies first of all engage themselves to strive for liberation for the poor and the oppressed. In doing this, the Bible and the message of Jesus Christ are read as sources of God's liberating power: doing theology thus means focusing on the liberating and transformative power of biblical texts and the tradition. In this sense, liberation theologies' interpretations of tradition would benefit from a Deleuzian reading of tradition as the creative repetition to which I referred in the previous chapter. Obviously, I will focus on the nature of liberation theologies more thoroughly in the second part of this chapter.

In what follows, the two 'sides' of liberation will be highlighted – in Deleuze as well as in theology. Both the destructive component of liberation (what are we against?) and the constructive or transformative side of it (what is our vision?) are necessarily elaborated on in order to draw a more fully realized view of this project of liberation. It will be a rather radical and even surprising kind of liberation, not aimed at individuals but at collectivities; not aimed at developing a new ideology that can revolt against the old one but at formulating strategies and tactics to *escape* from all sorts of ideologies – for this is the only way in which we can really escape from the capitalist ideology or 'axiomatic', as Deleuze and Guattari call it.

Political Deleuze

To a certain extent, Deleuze's politics remain quite hidden in his books, even in those he wrote with Guattari: it is very difficult, if not impossible, to trace a clear-cut concrete political programme from these books. As a consequence, it is impossible to describe a well-defined 'Deleuzian politics'. In this first part of the chapter, I choose to present Deleuze's philosophy as a project of liberation in the two senses described above. In my opinion, this presentation at the same time highlights the most significant characteristics of Deleuze's political thought.

Indeed, it is clear that Deleuze was against representation from the outset of his philosophical project. In the configuration of the capitalist society, representation is translated or expresses itself as 'the axiomatic'. In *Anti-Oedipus*, Deleuze and Guattari invent 'schizoanalysis' as an alternative to the capitalism-endorsing psychoanalysis to liberate desire from the individual, human beings, representation and the axioms of the capitalist society more broadly. Eight years later, in *A Thousand Plateaus*, their constructive project of liberation is described as 'minor politics' or 'micropolitics'. I will identify the three main tasks of schizoanalysis with aspects of micropolitics that also return in *A Thousand Plateaus*: the focus on the molecular and minorities, the process of deterritorialization and the creation of desiring machines or assemblages (new kinds of communities). Although *Anti-Oedipus* is interpreted as a book of revolution, while *A Thousand Plateaus* has a more modest goal, a political engagement is strongly and obviously present in both books.

What is Deleuze against?

At the level of metaphysics, one could say that Deleuze is against *representation*. From a more social angle, it could be stated that Deleuze is against the *axiomatic*. Indeed, the axiomatic is the form which representation adopts in our contemporary, capitalist society. For Deleuze and Guattari, capitalism is the latest great form of social organization (after the savage and the feudal organizations of society), and it differs from the previous forms in that it uses axioms (that correspond to function) to organize society instead of 'codes' (corresponding to meaning) to structure desire. I will return to Deleuze and Guattari's treatment of capitalism later in this chapter.

Liberation from representation

Thinking on a plane of immanence implies liberation from the logic of representation, which is, itself, a logic of transcendence, as has already become clear in Chapter 1. The necessary project entails a liberation from the world of representation, which instead moves towards an understanding of being as a purely immanent dynamic. This 'metaphysical' liberation has already been interpreted as a spiritual project in which true life can only be lived if the complexity of reality is conceived as it is: not in terms of identity, organization or institution but in terms of movements, velocity, intensity and power. At first sight, it might seem that the dynamics of being are somewhat indifferent to particular events – things happen in the flow of being and then they pass. Deleuze's account of immanent being could resemble an uncritical stream of intensities, in which actual events are unimportant and all particularities are absorbed in the great energetic 'fold' of being. At the same time, though, this spiritual project implies a certain underlying ethics. It is dependent on a vision of a liberated Being, a world in which there are no longer hierarchies and in which individuality is transcended in favour of a new collectivity, a 'people to come' (WP, 109). For Deleuze and Guattari, the creative is inextricably interconnected with the social and the political.

From the perspective of metaphysics, in a philosophy of transcendence, ethics (in this manifestation called morality) is detached from and prevails over being (the latter often being interpreted as the immanent, blind, biological struggle to survive). Conversely, for Deleuze as representative of a philosophy of immanence, ontology *is* ethics. What is more, only an immanent ethics, coming forth from the creativity of Being itself, is capable of avoiding the logic of representation, its lack of creativity and its consequential hierarchies.

In this respect, one can also understand why Deleuze's concept of difference does not seem to end in a nonstop respect for the concrete other – difference for him the other is 'just' the movement of being; no other cannot transcend another. Defining difference or transcendence as concrete differences between human beings would again root difference in an underlying principle of identity (we are all human beings), and this is exactly what Deleuze is trying to escape from. And perhaps the Deleuzian concept of difference, one that is not based on identity, pays more respect to diversity among beings – not only human beings but also, for example, animals and plants. So, as Deleuze scholar Ronald Bogue writes, 'Although Deleuze does not develop a formal ethics as a discrete component of his philosophy, there is a sense in which the ethical permeates all his work',[3] starting with his battle against representation.

Liberation from the axiomatic

As indicated above, Deleuze's ethics (and politics) circle around the notion of desire. This is very different from 'usual' political projects that centre on the notion of subjectivity, the state or other visible political bodies of power. Focusing on the notion of desire gives Deleuze and Guattari's ethics a range that goes deeper than those that limit themselves to the public or social domain. Indeed, when stripped of their connection to the economy of desire and relegated to the domain of the social, ethics risk becoming both relative and fetishized – matters of personal choice or preference that are often grounded only in their actual effect on ourselves. Focusing on the notion of desire as an ontological drive ensures that such ethics will not become matters of social capital or become captivated in a system of Morality again. Together, Philip Goodchild remarks, the two philosophers, 'address Capital in the ontological dimension appropriate to it'.[4] Indeed, desire, for Deleuze and Guattari, no longer belongs to the unconscious being of an individual; it is a *productive force* beyond human beings that is expressed in and between bodies and/or machines. Desire thus becomes a social force that is not bound to the individual.

The key question of our time, Deleuze said in an interview, is how we got to the point that we desire our own servitude. Underneath the visible power that exerts its force, there is the desire that organizes it, and it is this desire that 'organizes the system of repression' (DI, 264). The central political question is the mystery of voluntary subservience (*why* do we collectively tolerate power?)[5]. The answer to that question is that we tolerate, even actively participate and reify our own subservience because desire is captivated in the axiomatic of capitalism. How does the axiomatic work? Deleuze and Guattari's analysis of capitalist society in *Anti-Oedipus* and of the axiomatic in *A Thousand Plateaus* helps us to understand how the mechanisms of oppression within capitalism work and how we could possibly escape from them.

The odd thing about the capitalist dynamic – although nowadays, it is no longer altogether surprising – is that its very core consists of inducing and then patching up *crises*. What provokes a crisis in capitalism is the dynamics of deterritorialization that is central to it. Indeed, at first sight, capitalism is all about freeing our desires, creating flows that can go all directions: it is a massive movement of 'decoding', of removing the code from a flux. 'While decoding doubtless means understanding and translating a code, it also means destroying the code as such, assigning it an archaic, folkloric, or residual function' (AO, 266). Whereas previous forms of organizing our societies were based on the practices of coding and even overcoding (overloading things and relations with *meaning* and regulations), capitalism removes all codes by functionalizing everything, ripping them out of their contexts and mobilizing them for the accumulation of capital. What emerges are 'decoded flows':

> Flows of property that is sold, flows of money that circulates, flows of production and means of production making ready in the shadows, flows of workers becoming deterritorialized: the encounter of all these flows will be necessary – their conjunction, and their reaction to one another – and the contingent nature of this encounter, this conjunction, and this reaction, which occur one time – in order for capitalism to be born. (AO, 244)

Capitalism constitutes a plane of immanence. There is no longer a transcendent code which regulates its flows. Nevertheless, a new immanent regulatory principle simultaneously, perhaps inevitably, emerges on the capitalist plane of immanence: the principle of axiomatization. Axioms, a kind of abstract, functional 'rules' that remain indifferent to the specificity of the domain they try to order, are invented ad hoc, as answers to a particular economic situation, their aim always being to avoid what Marx calls the 'tendency to a falling rate of profit' (AO, 248). One of the fundamental phenomena in capitalism is the *'transformation of the surplus value of code into a surplus value of flux'* (AO, 248). Instead of overcoding, capitalism tries to accumulate the value of (monetary) flux. A good example of this phenomenon in action is the double function of the bank: on the one hand, banks provide money as means of payment (wages for delivered labour), but on the other hand, they also serve as structures of financing that are basically, at their core, mere edifices that exist to propagate the artificial creation of surplus value of capital. This form of 'metaproduction' is necessary to maintain the capitalist ideal of accumulation. It is no longer focused on the production of goods out of raw materials but is situated at the level of the nonmaterial (the sale of services, e.g. credit).[6] Financing the capitalist system is necessary to avoid the aforementioned falling rate of profit: the flow of money must be energized and fed constantly in order for it to keep flowing and growing. However, the downside of this continuous demand for accumulation of capital is an *increasing amount of debt*. The mechanism of creating more and more debts in order to maintain the surplus value of a flux will eventually become a form of what Deleuze and Guattari call 'anti-production'. It is this movement of anti-production that the logic of capitalism needs to survive, but which simultaneously ensures that capitalism can never be, in reality, a politics of liberation, despite its initial movement towards deterritorialization.

Another agent of anti-production is the State. If banks can no longer provide this 'credit money', then the State (within a capitalist logic) must and will do so. One would assume at first that States no longer play any role in this dynamic of abstract monetary flow.

> When the flows reach this capitalist threshold of decoding and deterritorialization (naked labor, independent capital), it seems that there is no longer need for a State, for distinct juridical and political domination, in order to ensure appropriation, which has become

directly economic. The economy constitutes a worldwide axiomatic, a "universal cosmopolitan energy which overflows every restriction and bond", a mobile and convertible substance "such as the total value of annual production". Today we can depict an enormous, so-called stateless, monetary mass that circulates through foreign exchange and across borders, eluding control by the States, forming a multinational ecumenical organization, constituting a de facto supranational power untouched by governmental decisions. (ATP, 500–1)

It is true indeed that the financial flows, the flows of workers and other flows ignore the territory of the State. The British economist and philosopher Noreena Hertz has convincingly demonstrated the declining role of the State. In *The Silent Takeover*, she describes how corporations have increasingly taken over the many of the powers of the State. One needs to look no further than the ever growing number of calls from around the world for the privatization of existing government service. However, history has proven Deleuze and Guattari right when they noticed that the State has neither disappeared nor diminished at all in capitalist society but that it has, instead, simply acquired a new role.

> Thus the States, in capitalism, are not canceled out but change form and take on a new meaning: models of realization for a worldwide axiomatic that exceeds them. (. . .) It is thus proper to State deterritorialization to moderate the superior deterritorialization of capital and to provide the latter with compensatory reterritorializations. (ATP, 502)

Ironically, as a force of anti-production, the State has become the 'doctor' of the economy. Far from being a transcendent organ of institutions that regulate society, the State has become an immanent regulator that helps to maintain the capitalist dynamic by being a player on the field. By guaranteeing real value for the credit money of banks, the State makes sure that the rate of profit does not fall too deeply (thus ensuring that more debt can be manufactured). The State picks up the surplus produced by this capitalist logic, and in the process, it both legitimates itself and ensures its continued existence.

The State 'pervades all production and becomes coextensive with it' (AO, 271). The State functions as a corrective mechanism to the deterritorializing and abstract flow of capital. It ties this down, as it were, in order to once again make itself relevant. In this way, the State absorbs the surplus value of fluxes (AO, 255).

> Bank credit effects a demonization or dematerialization of money, and is based on the circulation of drafts instead of the circulation of money. (...) The State as a regulator ensures a principle of convertibility of this credit money, either directly by tying it to gold, or indirectly through a mode of centralization that comprises a guarantor of the credit, a uniform interest rate, a unity of capital markets, etc. (AO, 249)

What becomes obvious in this dynamic is that the flows and fluxes that capitalism engenders are, in fact, infinitely self-propagating. Because of the perpetuating process of decoding and deterritorializing, capitalism has no external limits to its logic; the only limit of capitalism is an internal one, namely capital itself. And since that limit is constantly moved up by accumulation and creation of surplus value, it is not an absolute limit but only a relative one. As such, crises serve as the means by which capitalism is able to expand its limits further. Crises are 'the means immanent to the capitalist mode of production' (AO, 251). Could it be, though, that we are approaching a new kind of external limit, namely the complete depletion of natural supplies? This is, of course, a material limit, and one could ask oneself whether capitalism will not find a new, non-material source to guarantee or back up its financing system. Capitalism has a great co-opting power; its axiomatic is very wide and englobing (AO, 257). But as earthly resources become exhausted and overpopulation becomes a fact, the crises of capitalism will likely become larger and larger. More and more, the physical and psychical limits of human beings living and working within capitalist societies are also accumulating and beginning to cause epidemics of depression, burn-outs and other 'malfunctionings'.

At this point, Deleuze and Guattari do identify an external limit of capitalism – the only one that exists, in their view, and thus, the only means of escaping capitalism: schizophrenia.

The schizophrenic way, as opposed to the oedipal principle that supports capitalism, is the only possible revolutionary way forward according to Deleuze and Guattari. But if one wished to draw back from the global economy, the question remains whether such an endeavour is even possible. However, 'there is but one centered world market, the capitalist one, in which even the so-called socialist countries participate' (ATP, 482). All States and social structures become isomorphic. This phenomenon is clearly visible in the way that both rightist and leftist political parties now ideologically move towards the centre. Moreover, capitalism expels its most deterritorialized product: the schizophrenic. It tries to control schizophrenics by labelling them as ill, and in its phobia of that illness, it watches anxiously even over its artists and scientists (AO, 266). This is why Deleuze and Guattari propose a movement in the opposite direction: to go even further into and towards the movements of decoding and deterritorializing in order to escape capitalist control mechanisms that are now nearly omnipresent:

> Which is the revolutionary path? (. . .) Might it be to go in the opposite direction? To go still further, that is, in the movement of the market, of decoding and deterritorialization? For perhaps the flows are not yet deterritorialized enough, not decoded enough, from the viewpoint of a theory and a practice of highly schizophrenic character. Not to withdraw from the process, but to go further, to "accelerate the process," as Nietzsche put it: in this matter, the truth is that we haven't seen anything yet. (AO, 260)

'Schizoanalysis' brings us to the margins of capitalism. In opposition to psychoanalysis, schizoanalysis is aimed at engendering a *collective* liberation. At the edges of capitalism, the subject too is decoded and deterritorialized: it falls apart into a multiplicity of particles, and the desire that is released by this deterritorialization can be used to form new assemblages or machines. The key to revolution lies in the periphery, in the minorities that are needed by capitalism but are also feared: capitalism functions as a constant dynamics of broadening limits. The capitalist logic encourages flows to deterritorialize, to become more and more abstract so that they facilitate the workings of capitalism: abstract flows allow interchangeability, a quality needed to maximize chances for profit. On the other hand, capitalist's severe axiomatics tie the deterritorialized flows to a mechanism of control. But in order to maintain this control, capitalism constantly has to invent new axioms to adapt to the decoded flows. So although schizophrenia as absolute deterritorialization is the normal tendency of the capitalist logic, it is completed by the countermovement of axiomatization. Capitalism 'has an exterior limit that is schizophrenia, that is, the absolute decoding of flows, but it functions only by pushing back and exorcising this limit' (AO, 271).

Because of the continuous movement of deterritorialization, which goes from the centre to the periphery – or from the developed countries to the underdeveloped ones – the gap between poor and rich constantly enlarges. It is not the case that capitalism expels underdeveloped regions from its logic; to the contrary, capitalism *needs* underdeveloped countries in order to control its falling profit range by exporting its processes of production. This set of principles is called the 'dependency theory', a Marxist insight that was endorsed by liberation theologians from the beginning of the movement. In principle, for capitalism, everyone is equal – the system makes no distinction between people based on gender, race and so on. The position of the poor within that system, however, is somewhat different: they are not excluded, but used, just like the rich are also used, to accumulate capital. The only difference between people is created by the direction of the flow of money. The 'advantage' of being on the margins is that there is at least the possibility of escape from the double logic of capitalism, and the chances to escape increase as capitalism is forced to broaden its limits. The fact that, nowadays, one crisis follows the other at a more and more rapid rate could be interpreted as a sign that capitalism is reaching its external limit. States have more and more difficulty backing up the system, saving the banks, and it is becoming more and more difficult to create new axioms to control the flows of money that have gone astray.

Minor politics

From what I described above, it has become clear that the liberation from representation and from the axiomatic is not a matter that exists at the level of the individual subject, but it is rather a matter of the collective – although collectivity does not indicate a collection of human beings. By making desire an impersonal power, Deleuze advocates a liberation from humanism too. Indeed, when we investigate his constructive politics of liberation, his vision or alternative, three key features can be discerned in which human beings no longer play a key role as agents of resistance against a system. Philip Goodchild identifies in this way of thinking a triple liberation from humanism.[7] First, political assemblages are no longer associations of humans for the mastery of nature. Assemblages can consist of all sorts of 'material', of human but also incorporeal components, living and nonliving. Second, thought is liberated from consciousness and representation. It has become an experiment, a practice of immanent critique. The third and most significant liberation from humanism has already been hinted at in my discussion of capitalism. The process of abstraction of flows entails a decentring of the subject, which becomes schizophrenic if not strictly controlled. 'In capitalism, the imperial subjects of the signifying regime and the sovereign subjects of the postsignifying regime are both reproduced and undermined by the schizophrenic subject. Capitalism, as a new social machine and new mode of representation, produces a post-humanist subjectivity'.[8]

Deprived of subjectivity, minor politics has to create another 'agent' for its politics. The 'lines of escape' that detach from the capitalist logic have to gather again on another plane, Deleuze contends. 'This is precisely the problem facing marginal groups: to make all the lines of escape connect up on a revolutionary plane. Within capitalism, then, these lines of escape take on a new character, and a new kind of revolutionary potential' (DI, 270). It is on this revolutionary plane that new assemblages can be created, assemblages that do not operate through a logic of representation and can thereby invent new kinds of collective politics.

In the following paragraphs, I will discuss Deleuze and Guattari's minor politics as a model of liberation in which I discern three components: minorities or margins as the place where the act of liberation starts; the process of deterritorialization by which these minorities can escape the capitalist system; and the new assemblages they form on their revolutionary plane. The outcome of an attempt to escape, however, is always insecure. Kenneth Surin's words: 'Deleuze and Guattari insist that there are no pregiven laws to shape or entail this outcome; only struggle, and failures always accompany successes in struggle, can do this'.[9] One can only hope that the movement becomes more widespread, that it multiplies and becomes larger, that it forms a growing rhizome. But there are no guarantees, and success can definitely not be measured by popularity or recognition.[10]

Minorities and micropolitics

Becoming-minoritarian, as we saw in Chapter 2, is a step in the process of becoming more and more impersonal and detached from representations. A minority is not defined by the number of its members but by its position: minorities occupy the non-dominant, powerless positions, at the margins of the system. Not only is becoming-minoritarian a spiritual process, it is also political in nature: 'Becoming-minoritarian is a political affair and necessitates a labor of power (*puissance*), and active micropolitics' (ATP, 322). If schizoanalysis was a way of analyzing the capitalist regime in order to escape from it, then micropolitics is the constructive political action that comes forth from the margins of capitalism. Indeed, only minorities can escape from axioms. This does not necessarily mean that the role of macropolitics is removed in the struggle against the capitalist axiomatic; it does mean, however, that this struggle must start at the level of micropolitics, a politics driven by desire that is constantly moving. This notion directly opposes the way Deleuze and Guattari conceive of macropolitics, an essentially conservative politics that is aimed at the conservation of the existing relations and the affirmation of her dominance. The reason Deleuze and Guattari turn to the level of the minor is that they want to demonstrate that binary oppositions and other such categories no longer function at this level. Binarities on a microlevel, for example, become molecular assemblages that are essentially different from the categories to which they belong in on the macrolevel. 'If we consider the great binary aggregates, such as the sexes or classes, it is evident that they also cross over into molecular assemblages of a different nature' (ATP, 235). The two sexes become 'a thousand tiny sexes' at the level of micropolitics (ATP, 235). The logic of representation is *not sufficient* to define a problem of a category; it is not able to grasp reality in all its complexity. There is, indeed, always something that escapes categorization: 'There is always something that flows or flees, that escapes the binary organizations, the resonance apparatus, and the overcoding machine' (ATP, 238). This is why ultimately the logic of capitalism is only fully understandable, and changeable, at the level of micropolitics – when it is understood as a *captive of desire* and not as a (macropolitical) ideology. As revolutionary movements, minorities challenge the world wide axiomatic (ATP, 521). By their very existence, they are able to have an effect on the macropolitical level. 'It is by leaving the plan(e) of capital, and never ceasing to leave it, that a mass becomes increasingly revolutionary and destroys the dominant equilibrium of the denumerable sets' (ATP, 521). Indeed, in order to be anything at all, molecular movements have to return to molar (or macropolitical) organizations, in order to reorganize their segments (ATP, 238–9).

Reality also confirms the need to couple the micro to the macrolevel. At first sight, one could read micropolitics as a plea for a return to the local, a return that many anti-globalist thinkers and movements have supported. Naomi Klein, for example, strives for local communities' right to organize and plan their community as a whole.[11] She works towards a picture of one world with many worlds in it. Alas, these communities also run the risk of being pervaded with the logic of capital. The real problem is, Buchanan and Parr note, that 'the axiomatic is able to treat all forms of organisation as its model of realization',[12] however small these communities may be. It is therefore necessary for a community, Buchanan and Parr conclude, to obtain the right to determine what can and cannot be a model of realization of a non-capitalist society. This is a matter of governmental macropolitics, but in order to see how macropolitics could and should be changed, we need the creative dynamics of micropolitics – we need to escape the logic of capitalism. This can only be done by the process of deterritorialization.

Deterritorialization

The process of deterritorialization has already been described in the section on axiomatics. It is a process that belongs to the core of the capitalist logic but also enables minorities to escape. Spiritually spoken, it is a process of what Eckhart calls *Abgeschiedenheit*, a process of decoding in which all meaning and identity are left behind, until the only driving force remains: desire. In the process of deterritorialization, it is possible to discern three 'actors': the territory from which something is detached, the process of detaching/deterritorialization and the inevitable process of reterritorialization. To say it with an example used by Deleuze and Guattari: 'The merchant buys in a territory, deterritorializes products into commodities, and is reterritorialized on commercial circuits' (WP, 68). Reterritorialization does not necessarily mean a return to the old territory; it also entails new kinds of organizations or assemblages that emerge. In the first place, deterritorialization is a process of unsettlement, of disruption. As such, it is part of the capitalist logic of decoding flows of production. But as I mentioned earlier, deterritorialization in the context of capitalism brings with it an accumulation not only of capital, but also of debt. Debt induces a mechanism of anti-production, because it creates dependency. A concrete investigation of how this mechanism of capital and debt works can be found in Noreena Hertz's book *I.O.U: The Debt Threat and Why We Must Defuse It*.[13] During the Cold War, both camps tried to enlarge their range of influence by lending large amounts of money, mostly to developing countries, without asking themselves whether there was a democratic regime in that particular state. When debts suddenly had to be refunded after the Cold War, the developing countries got into trouble. To this day, for many countries, the refunding of the debts is paid at the cost of the interests and the development of the local inhabitants. In addition, after '9/11', the United States once again used the same strategy: in exchange for support in their 'war against terrorism', many undemocratic states (such as Pakistan, at the time led by Musharraf) received loans from the United States. Not only states but also organizations such as the World Bank and the IMF impose large amounts of debts to developing countries. Hertz consequently pleas for a complete remission of debt for the world's poorest countries. As for the cause of these mechanisms of dependency, Hertz points to the unbridled greed of capitalism. For her, capitalism must be tamed, not only by the state (macropolitical structures) but also from the bottom up, by means of all sorts of action groups (in *The Silent Takeover*, she mentions consumer protests, e-mail networks and environmental activism in this context): in other words, by micropolitics.

Although Deleuze and Guattari do not deny the necessity of macropolitics, liberation for them is only possible through micropolitics and through an ongoing process of deterritorialization.

Deterritorialization liberates the desire that lies beneath codes. This desire can be re-coded in endless ways, but it can also remain free and flowing at an infinite velocity and can drive in the direction of schizophrenia. In this sense, deterritorialization is a way of counter-actualization, of bringing processes on the virtual plane of immanence back to where they can be creative again. In relation to music and language, Deleuze and Guattari describe deterritorialization as follows: 'Everywhere, organized music is traversed by a line of abolition – just as a language of sense is traversed by a line of escape – in order to liberate a living and expressive material that speaks for itself and has no need of being put into a form' (K, 21).

Assemblages

Deleuze's politics of liberation is a form of *collective liberation*. More specifically, it is certainly not a matter of the individual; liberation is liberation of the nondenumerable minority. It is not about numbers but about the movement of a collective body of minorities out of the capitalist axiomatic. The transition towards a postcapitalist society that Deleuze and Guattari envision requires a powerful collective engagement – a strong social movement that operates independently from state structures – at the margins of 'the system'. Kenneth Surin calls this a process of 'delinking' from the capitalist economy of the centre. But there are no fixed rules of delinking, 'there are no pregiven laws to shape or entail this [revolutionary project of surmounting capitalism]; only struggle, and failures always accompany successes in struggle, can do this'.[14] In this vision, the state as a transcendent provider of codes and rules can no longer subsist. Neither is this collective liberation an affair of the 'family' (an agglomerate used by the capitalist logic to strengthen its control over desire).

An assemblage is the concept by which Deleuze and Guattari imagine new forms of community, of a collective subjectivity. What might such a community concretely look like? It might be risky, to be sure, to think about assemblages in an all-too-concrete way because of the inherent danger present in the act of making such bodies visible, of representing them. However, concreteness is also something we can demand of Deleuze's political project. If you claim that your metaphysics is practical, your ethics and political vision must be concrete. Thinking about existing political assemblages today, Buchanan and Parr refer to the communities of indigenous people and more specifically to the Zapatistas in Mexico:

> For Deleuze and Guattari, the nondenumerable [minority] refers to the power to ask one's own questions, to form one's own problematics, and, more particularly, to define the conditions under which a satisfactory answer or response to these questions and problems might be obtained. Today, after so many centuries of suffering and silence, it is the indigenous peoples of the world who are showing the rest of us how potent this power can be.[15]

In my opinion, The 'Indignados' movement that emerged in the Summer of 2011 is another strong example of what an assemblage might look like. To me, the Indignados (Spanish for 'indignants') are a perfect example of a new kind of community that fits with Deleuze and Guattari's understanding of minorities and assemblages. Moreover, this could be the form that communities will embody in the future – the question will be whether they succeed in escaping the axioms of capitalism or not. It is a global community, not bound to any kind of locality, which is always on the move, either 'virtually' (at the level of the internet) or actually (the Indignados' pilgrimage from Madrid to Brussels). The group has no fixed number of members; people join it, others leave it. There is no leader, no spokesman in the assemblage of the Indignados. But they also have a destructive element within them. Their mere presence is their statement; the way they penetrate society is a disturbing element. The established political world hurries to formulate an answer to the question of their presence, or at least to form a way of 'understanding these young people', but in fact does not know where to begin with these untamed masses. It is remarkable that this assemblage is constituted by young people. Most do not work; they are not yet fully absorbed in the capitalist process of production; they do not yet participate consciously in the system but are situated in the margins of it. As a consequence, they might still have the ability to escape from it.

Generally, we could conclude that an assemblage is not founded on a common identity of its composing elements. To the contrary, it is a wholly contingent conjunction of bodies (human and non-human alike), a collection of dissimilars that coincide but that also share a 'belief in this world'. In relation to the theological appreciation of this concept Deleuzian concept, it can already be noted that this kind of community will have large repercussions on the concept of Christian identity because it is precisely nót a shared identity that brings different components of an assemblage together or binds them together.

Liberation theologies

To the German protestant liberation theologian Dorothee Sölle, mysticism and revolt are inextricably connected to each other.[16] Despite the Christian inclination to glorify the *vita contemplativa* above a *vita activa*, the greatest mystics (among them Meister Eckhart) have always contested this distinction.

The mystical desire for God urges a commitment to the world or rather, an engagement to *change* the world. Both mysticism and revolt imply a negative relation to the world as it is, a relation that expresses itself in a withdrawal from this world, a revolt or a pursuit of reformation (which expresses the positive will to contribute to constructive changes in this world). The unity of mysticism and revolt indicates that the resistance is rooted in a desire for God; the revolt is driven by a vision of liberation. For Sölle, mystical theology is always liberation theology.

Referring to Chapter 2, we could say that both elements – mysticism and revolt – are present in Deleuze's thought. The word 'mysticism' then indicates a spiritual transformation, a loss of the self, or in Deleuzian terms: becoming-imperceptible and an absorption into the stream of being. It is a mysticism of Life. In the previous section, I demonstrated that Deleuze's spiritual metaphysics is deeply connected to a political engagement. Deleuze's thought could thus be said to contain all elements necessary to support a liberation theology. Of course, Deleuze's project of liberation is not based on the revelation of God in Christ, nor on the Bible. Nevertheless, remarkable similarities with Christian theology of liberation at the level of structure and content can be discerned in Deleuze.

Parallel with the previous paragraphs, I will first focus on what liberation theologies stand against. Their resistance can be defined as a resistance against oppression and sinful structures in society. Traditionally, Karl Marx' philosophical and economic analysis of capitalism was used to detect these structures of oppression. But after 1989, his theories lost a modicum of credibility[17] and were replaced during the two subsequent decades by an amalgam of postcolonialist, feminist, queer and other postmodern critical theories. Literature teaches us that the 'traditional' Christian theology of liberation that originated in Latin America in the 1960s and 1970s has resulted in an almost infinite number of separate 'liberation theologies', developed and lived in all parts of the world. In European postmodern theology, the political element was explicitly restored by the so-called Radical Orthodoxy movement that emerged in Great Britain in the nineties of the previous century. Still, Radical Orthodoxy is directed at the restoration of a neotraditional orthodoxy in which the Christian tradition is not really changed but rather retrieved from the past. Moreover, other than liberation theology, the political theology of the Radical Orthodoxy movement affirms no direct connection between historical, political actions and the reign of God.[18] For the Radically Orthodox, this is a matter of analogy.

My wager here is that Deleuze (and Guattari) could offer liberation theology a new kind of mediation by which the role of mediations itself in liberation theologies is thoroughly changed: apart from offering an analysis of society and capitalism to liberation theologies, Deleuze can also effectuate a radical reformulation of liberation theology as a whole. Thereby, liberation theologies could do more than '[integrate] a Marxist critique and programmatic into an already established theological framework'.[19] Indeed, all central concerns of liberation theologies – the preferential option for the poor, the revolt against structural forms of oppression, the understanding of theology as an orthopraxis and the vision of the kingdom of God and the Church – are challenged and could be renewed by a Deleuzian reading of them.

Oppression and structural sin

What do liberation theologies stand against or react to? What do we need to be liberated *from*? Traditional liberation theology was very clear about this: it fought against the mechanisms of oppression that were created by the logic of capitalism. Capitalism was considered a form of 'structural sin' that stood against the biblical vision of the reign of God. For liberation theologians, the world is not created by a transcendent God who made creation necessarily good; to the contrary, creation is pervaded by sin in every place and in every moment where and when creatures are oppressed or excluded. As a consequence, in its battle against oppression and exclusion, the capitalist system was attacked by its 'common' macropolitical alternative: socialism. However, since the defeat of socialism as a macropolitical alternative to capitalism and the following search for other alternatives, structures of oppression have been analyzed in a more differentiated and complex way. One realized that within structures of oppression, several layers can be discerned. It has become impossible now to speak about 'the poor' as a monolithic group of oppressed people who have no money. Not every man is equally poor. In fact, the word 'man' is already striking: it turns out that poverty is pre-eminently a *female* characteristic! But exclusion does not stop with the dualism man–woman. Among women, black women are generally much more disadvantaged than white women. Eventually, we end up at the level of sexuality, with the so-called 'queer theology', which is based on resistance to the most 'material', the deepest and most stubborn level of oppression (because it is mostly invisible), namely, the oppression of those men and women who are not heterosexual, who even challenge the categories of 'man' and 'woman' themselves: homosexuals, bisexuals and transgender people.

Discerning these different stages and levels of oppression, the battle of liberation theologies against exclusion has thus continued on another level that is more akin to Deleuze's micropolitical level than the alternative of socialism. However, this does not mean that liberation theologies with all their nuances and degrees of oppression do not revolt against capitalism anymore. To the contrary, by reconnecting all forms of exclusion to capitalism, queer theologian Marcella Althaus-Reid (1952–2009) demonstrates that liberation theologies today have not lost their focus – the common enemy that unites all forms of oppression is still named capitalism:

> All forms of capitalism are patriarchal derivatives, from the Democratic forms based on democracy as support system, to the functioning of the market and a cultural political platform based on Creation Theology, to Savage Capitalism, constituting economy as an end in itself. (. . .) The main characteristics of capitalism could be considered to be a binary economic epistemology, or a process of capital accumulation based on hierarchical exploitation (based on the man-woman heterosexual relation) and dominion produced through warfare and force.[20]

The citation above shows that the analysis of capitalism by Althaus-Reid goes beyond the level of ideology. In an almost Deleuzian/Guattarian fashion, she analyzes capitalism's existence as the result of a certain captivation of desire, namely a limiting of desire in a heterosexual axiomatic. It is this very subject that Deleuze and Guattari diagnosed as the Oedipal structuring of the social order.

As a logical consequence, the alternatives imagined and constructed are much more likely to engage with the 'molecular', on a smaller level, tracing and fighting *hidden* forms of oppression and thereby trying to make extinct all structural sin at its deepest materialist – economic and sexual – roots.

Theologies of liberation

Traditionally, Christian theologians and practitioners have made appeals to the transcendent God as the Liberator. But how can this Liberator and the surrounding theologies be reconciled to the completely immanent forms of liberation Deleuze creates and formulates? If we take a look at three central concerns of all liberation theologies, it turns out that it is very well possible to connect the tradition to the Deleuzian, immanent project of liberation, in which the liberating force comes from within rather than from above. It is important to note that this apparent 'filling in' of liberation theology's core characteristics with a Deleuzian content is not just an exercise free of all engagement. As I will try to demonstrate, liberation theologies need a mediation, an adequate analysis of structures of oppression and of capitalism, not only for the analysis' sake but also for the development of their alternatives. Without such a mediation, liberation theologies too run the risk to be absorbed by the logic of capitalism, just as virtually any other organization or project does. Indeed, it cannot be denied that even the IMF would support the option for the poor and the project of liberation.[21] Capitalism, Deleuze has shown, is initially all about liberation (of desire, of flows)! In this respect, contemporary liberation theologian Ivan Petrella has argued for the need of strong mediations:

> I posit that liberation theology's concepts remain empty without a role for the social sciences in the construction of historical projects. Liberation theology needs to realize that concepts such as the preferential option for the poor and liberation reveal little about the way life chances and social resources may be theoretically approached and institutionally realized.[22]

Parallel with the first part of this chapter, I will unfold the constructive programme of liberation theologies on the basis of three of its main characteristics: the preferential option for the poor, the orthopraxis of liberation and the vision of the kingdom of God on earth and community. Also regarding their content, these characteristics are parallel with the ones I highlighted in Deleuze's political aspirations.

The option for the poor – 'becoming-poor'

The most important and 'famous' characteristic of every liberation theology is its so-called 'preferential option for the poor', the engagement to do theology from the perspective of the poor, and in this theology, to strive for liberation for the poor. In the 'classical' liberation theology of the 1960s and 70s, the poor were identified with the *socio-economic poor* on the one hand – a poverty that results from the logic of capitalism – and the *evangelical poor* on the other hand: all people who do not look for the centre of their existence within themselves but in God; all creatures who live at the service of God.[23] Although within liberation theologies today, the poor are defined in a much more differentiated way (as explained above), the two characteristics of exclusion on one side and hierarchical power on the other remain present. But when laid aside in favour of Deleuze's concept of the minority and the process of becoming-minoritarian, the true revolutionary potential of the poor becomes clear. The concept of 'becoming-poor' can be put forward as an indispensable new concept of a liberation theology inspired by Deleuze.

Indeed, the poor can be interpreted as different minorities. Being poor and becoming poor are not in the first place about material possessions but about *positions*: a creature that is poor is dominated by a despot or by a system that controls its freedom and desire. We should keep in mind that a minority does not indicate a minority in number but rather what can be described as a 'minority in meaning': within the oppressive system, the poor are denied all forms of subjectivity and identity.

However, just like in Deleuze's thought, in liberation theology, the poor also have a positive meaning. The Bible praises the 'poor in spirit' (Matthew 5:3), just like Deleuze's spiritual project calls for becoming-minoritarian.

The concept of becoming-poor gives the poor a renewed power. They are no longer in a position of 'the victim'. To the contrary, it is only through them that liberation can be reached: they are situated in the locus of potential liberation. The poor are the primary agents of social change. Of course, this does not mean that 'we', middleclass or rich people, should envy the poor for their privileged position as possible agents and initiators of a movement of spiritual and political liberation. This liberating process is a tough task that requires minorities to give up their personal and subjective interests in order to form a collective subjectivity that is able to break through and disturb the centre. Becoming-poor is not only a concept that expresses the power of the poor, it is a *universal* call to everyone to become poor, to escape from oppressive structures such as capitalism and to move towards the margins. In the following, I will discuss some tactics that could support such becoming-poor of everything and everyone.

Orthopraxis of liberation: Tactics and strategies

Michel De Certeau articulated a significant difference between 'strategies' and 'tactics' in the context of his philosophy of 'everyday life', defining strategy as 'the calculation (or manipulation) of power relationships that become possible as soon as a subject with will and power (a business, an army, a city, a scientific institution) can be isolated'.[24] In other words, strategy implies a limited territory – it implies an already strong subject that appropriates a certain amount of power for itself. Tactics, on the contrary, are 'the art of the weak': it cannot start from a limited locus because the poor have no 'position' in society. The poor have no 'place of their own' from which a strategy could be developed.[25]

In order for tactics not to be embraced by the capitalist logic again (for this is the great danger with any kind of movement, and as before, which decent citizen would not agree with an option for the poor?), the tactics of liberation theology could adopt Deleuze's tactics of extreme deterritorialization. This means that liberation theology would primarily leave the domain of ideologies and macropolitics in order to develop tactics of resistance in 'everyday life'.[26]

A concrete example of theological tactics from the domain of queer theology is Althaus-Reid's development of what could be called a 'flowing Christology'.[27] In relation to the meaning, or rather the functioning of Christ (as a liberator) in queer theology, Althaus-Reid executes a deterritorialization of traditional Christology by first questioning the heteronormativity present in our traditional understandings of Jesus Christ. For Althaus-Reid, Christ is an *event* in which politics and spirituality converge. This event is the point of departure for depatriarchizing the whole of Christianity, and as such, the key to any deterritorialization of a patriarchal form of Christianity (the link with capitalism has been explained above).

Against the traditional interpretation of Christ as a God-man, interpreted as a male construct, Althaus-Reid is looking for a 'Christology that encourages all flowing'[28] – an alternative Christology that is constantly evolving and changing, a Christology of 'becoming-Christ' as it were. Jesus Christ is deterritorialized from his context because he was limited by it: 'As God/man he was subjected to cultural and epochal elements which he did not succeed totally in transcending'.[29] The only possible conclusion from this insight is that even Jesus Christ has been involved during his life in a process of 'Becoming-Christ', a process that is still going on today. Jesus is 'becoming-Christ', for example, in a community of poor women (this is already the case in the Bible, e.g. in the story of the Samaritan woman in John 4): here, a community of poor women (or in general, of a minority) is a catalyst for Jesus to become Christ. As such, Christ escapes the yoke of heteronormativity: Christ is neither man nor woman, 'he' is *community*. In other words, the differentiation of the male, still heterosexually oriented Jesus of Nazareth into a desexualized Christ results in the interpretation of Christ as a community of the poor. This is not a strategy but a tactic by which a community of the poor can acquire consciousness of their strength and their capacity to transform normative frameworks, such as the heteronormative interpretation of Jesus Christ, which is itself a part of a patriarchally organized society and which supports the logic of capitalism.

The Kingdom of God on earth: Church and community

The church is the visible institution that embodies the presence of God on earth and allows believers to live their faith in community. How can this be an instrument for liberation? In his book *Liberation Theology After the End of History*, Daniel Bell develops an ecclesiology inspired by (among others) Deleuze's analysis of capitalism. Bell agrees with Deleuze that capitalism is best analyzed at the level of ontology, as a problem of desire. He thus wants to abandon the terrain of ideology and put forward the Christian account of desire, which is, in his view, a perfect alternative in the battle against capitalism. In fact, for Bell, the Christian economy of desire is the only alternative that allows us to escape from the logic of capitalism. 'Christianity is reclaimed as an ensemble of technologies that reforms or shapes desire in ways that counter the capitalist discipline of desire'.[30] Indeed, the cultivation of the desire for God, the passion and the search for God, has always been the driving force of every Christian. This desire was best formulated by Augustine with his famous expression that 'our hearts are restless until they rest in Thee'.

However, it is doubtful that Deleuze and Guattari would agree with this orientation of desire for God because it is specifically defined from a lack, and such lack is precisely what they try to avoid most. For Deleuze and Guattari, desire is the impersonal force of being that causes being to differentiate and to create. So if the desire for God is not to be defined from a lack, it should be equal with the love of God which is experienced by human beings and other creatures. Still, Bell does not seem to make this equation explicitly. He even interprets Christianity as a therapy: 'Christianity as a therapy of desire operates under the "burden" (which is a light one) of a direction that is given desire by virtue of its being the gift that is the desire of God'.[31] According to Bell, since Christianity offers an alternative logic of desire, it can also provide an alternative for the violent logic of capitalism. Bell finds this alternative not in a Christian account of justice but in the concept of forgiveness. 'Forgiveness is the name of the ensemble of technologies that God has graciously made available to humanity in Christian communities for the sake of healing desire of the madness that is capitalism'.[32] Forgiveness is a process that is always expressed in a relational context, so for Bell it is intrinsically linked to an ecclesiology. Through forgiveness, we are able to escape the violence of the capitalist order; we no longer feel the need to participate in it; we can turn from this logic of 'eye for an eye' and express God's overabundant love instead. But in order to perform this function, the church must regain a political power. In other words, the distinction between theology and politics should disappear.

> Only a more substantive ecclesiology, one that begins by collapsing the distinction between the theological and the social, between religion and politics, stands a chance of resisting capitalist discipline. This ecclesiology must reclaim the theological as a material, that is, as a fully social, political, economic reality. This ecclesiology will recognize the practice of faith as intrinsically – instead of derivatively – social, political, economic.[33]

Theology is a directly political matter. Bell wants to theorize what is already present in many basic communities in Latin America. These basic communities, with their decentralized politics, are real alternatives to the capitalist logic, 'as the state and civil society increasingly reveal their true nature as vassals of the capitalist order'.[34] The problem with Bell's understanding of the church is that it maintains a dichotomy between the so-called 'city of God' and the 'city of man'. In this sense, he is truly an heir of the Radical Orthodoxy movement, which strives to reinstall a neo-Augustinian world view. According to Petrella, the church is presented by Bell as the only body that can escape capitalism, because it is impossible that 'the spirit' should be 'corrupted'.[35]

What Bell actually does, however, is eliminate the role of a mediation for theology. He uses the mediation of Deleuze's philosophy to analyze capitalism as a problem of desire, but for the alternative, he ditches this mediation altogether, thereby isolating theology (and the church) once again from the domain of the social. Indeed, Bell's concept of the church is not at all changed by the analysis of society. Theology creates an analysis for itself. As John Milbank, the 'father' of the Radical Orthodoxy movement confirms, theology does not need the social sciences – it is in itself encompassing enough.[36] The alternative Bell presents eventually ends up sounding very 'republican'. As Petrella notes: 'politics is not radicalized but reduced to acts of social charity and the fostering of community'.[37]

In opposition to this view on ecclesiology, I would like to propose some initial steps in the development of an alternative view on church and community that are inspired by Deleuze's concept of the assemblage.[38] If we subscribe to Deleuze's theory of how to escape capitalist logic, our vision regarding the task of the church will be radically altered. Indeed, an assemblage is never a static structure but always a process: 'Its [the assemblage's] territoriality is only a first aspect; the other aspect is constituted by *lines of deterritorialization* that cut across it and carry it away' (ATP, 556). An assemblage has no fixed identity but is a contingent organization of accidental encounters. If the Indignados are a good example of an assemblage today, Jesus Christ and his apostles were the assemblage upon which Christianity was founded – although for an assemblage to be a foundation, the essence of the assemblage has to be corrupted so that it is, in fact, no assemblage anymore. Whereas Christianity is a visible system of rather static doctrines and institutions, Jesus and his apostles were always on the move and continually visited the most remote and poor areas (e.g. Galilee). In order to enter into an assemblage, Deleuze and Guattari write, one has to take up the 'speed', the 'intensity' of the assemblage (ATP, 337). It is not a matter of identity (the apostles were all very different men, with different professions and lives); it is a matter of becoming. As Wise puts it: 'We can enter into an assemblage through a process of taking up or taking on the particular relation of speed, slowness, effectivity and language which makes it up. (. . .) It is not a process of imitating but of *becoming*'.[39] A follower of Jesus Christ is asked to give up his or her identity in order to be taken up in real, divine life:

> If anyone would come after me, he must deny himself and take up his cross and follow me. For whoever wants to save his life will lose it, but whoever loses his life for me and for the gospel will save it. (Mark 8:34–5)

Picturing the church as an assemblage situates it in the domain of the molecular and the micropolitical. Churches can also emerge invisibly, and they can remain invisible (to macropolitics and the rest of society). But in order for the church to become a real space for resistance against the logic of capitalism, it has to abandon its structures of transcendence and hierarchy. Otherwise, there is no possibility that the church can become an assemblage of people who are not united through their identities but through a common concern and attempt to escape. Of course, assemblages create territories – if they did not, they could not give body to expression (ATP, 554–6). But assemblages that work must continuously move from one territory to another. They are always involved in processes of deterritorialization and reterritorialization – though reterritorialization is never the latest stage of an assemblage. Deterritorialization has to take place over and over again, because there are always leakages in a territory. If we apply the notion of this process to the narrative of Jesus, we will begin to notice the ways he constantly surrounded himself with different groups of people, sought out different 'settings' in which he performed his acts and always continued moving from one temporary territory to another. Jesus Christ always moved on, creating new communities that express the divine life (and by that very fact, revolt against the established order).

Inspired by Deleuze, the churches that liberation theologies could envision are radically different than the church as we now know it. A church assemblage is a non-hierarchical, temporary encounter of minorities, human and non-human, that function together in their resistance against the captivation of desire and the consequential forms of oppression and exploitation endemic to capitalist society. From the margins, a liberating church creates an immanent plane of resistance that can question and challenge established institutions and logics. Could it be that this kind of church is more akin to the testimony of Jesus Christ, that it is a more worthy 'repetition' of the Christ-event, than the church we know today?

Conclusion: The 'evangelical power' of Deleuze – towards a theology of life

I began writing this book with the idea that the work of Gilles Deleuze could help us formulate answers to what I consider to be *five urgent concerns for Christian theology today*. In my opinion, Deleuze effectuates a *liberation of theology*, a liberation Juan Luís Segundo already called for in the seventies[1] by providing theologies, and more specifically theologies of liberation – concepts and tools that oppressed individuals might use to liberate themselves from institutional, economic, social and other limits; concepts and tools to help them return to the creative event of Jesus Christ's life, by which they are initially inspired. An engagement with Deleuze's philosophy could co-create and support a theology that (re-)unites spirituality and revolt in a radical way. These five concerns are as much theological as they are 'simply' human, personal and, of course, also time-bound.

First, I believe that today there is a need for a non-confessional, immanent theology. In view of the critique of representation, it is problematic to confess to a personal, transcendent God who has revealed certain religious truths and doctrines to us. As I argued in the Chapter 1, an immanent theology could pay more respect to God *as God* than a transcendent theology could, precisely because it avoids the seduction of power, hierarchy and representation. In this respect, the entire book has been a plea for the *immanentization of theology*, one that breaks down the mechanisms of representation and transcendence, one that brings God back into our lives – not as a higher being but as an omnipresent power in life on earth. A theology after Deleuze would indeed move in the direction of a pan(en)theism. Several theologies have already come forth – implicitly or explicitly – from a metaphysics of immanent dynamics of being: ecotheology, feminist theology, queer theology and other liberation theologies. Apart from being immanent, all these theologies are in essence engaged with the world. They are postsecular in that they wish to overcome the gap between theology and society, between the sacred and the so-called secular.

Second, there is an urge that longs for a *new kind of political theology*, or more specifically, for a new liberation theology that engages with the crises of today. The multiple crises of neoliberal capitalism and of the environment demand theological answers and actions. A strong mediation that can help theology to formulate the problem and to create alternatives is needed. Deleuze, I believe, provides in such a mediation. A theology after Deleuze will not refrain from exerting its critical function to offer an antidote for an overly consumerist society and will create a community of spirituality and revolt as a powerful repetition of Jesus' life. The critical function of such a theology, then, does not come forth from the revelation of a transcendent person but is rather a form of immanent, impersonal critique.

Third, in a non-confessional, immanent theology, there will be a need to rearticulate one's relationship with *tradition*. In Chapter 3, I presented a Deleuzian account of tradition as a repetition of the Christ-event that is not bound to its origins (the historical life and death of Jesus) but that is intrinsically aimed at the future. Deleuze could give us a concept of tradition in which history is no longer normative for truth, but in which the power of the event that is repeated (Christ's life) and the creativity that it engenders are the 'norm' for any kind of concrete practice, be it liturgical (in church) or ethical (in society).

In our time, there is also an urge to *rethink spirituality*. All too often, spirituality is either considered an elitist matter or a hyper-individualist experience – vague new age-sense. From a Deleuzian perspective, spirituality is not a matter of an individual in search for a God; to the contrary, it is a process in which an individual *becomes* a collectivity by connecting with the power of the divine life on the level of the virtual. Deleuze's subjectivity is thus a collective subjectivity, such as the community of poor women described by Althaus-Reid in the Chapter 4 (although we must bear in mind that a spiritual community is certainly not restricted to human beings).

This account of a collective subjectivity (or an assemblage) results in a *new concept of community*. Communities should not be based on a shared identity or shared characteristics of their members. What members of a community have in common is a vision of a better life, of a more divine life that is detached from all personal, economic and social limitations. However, this detachment does not imply a retreat out of the world. No, it implies, rather, a dynamic of constant revolt against all forms of captivation of desire by the social structures.

This positing of *theology as constant revolt*, or as a '*révolution permanente*', to speak using the term Deleuze and Guattari borrowed from Marx, finally demonstrates what can be called the 'evangelical power' of Deleuze. The Belgian Jesuit Louis Van Bladel discerned four aspects of evangelical power, which can easily be connected to characteristics of Deleuze's philosophy[2]: a critical, a uptopian, a constructive, and a spiritual power.

Deleuze's philosophy offers theology a *critical power* because it performs a total critique of the logic of representation and axiomatics and calls for resistance against all forms of oppression or limitation of desire; it contains a *utopian power*, not because Deleuze's thought is teleological in any way (the end always remains unsure and open), but because it is intrinsically aimed towards creativity and the future; furthermore, Deleuze's thinking has a great *constructive power*, in that it allows for the development of a positive metaphysical system – and a theology after Deleuze would definitely be a constructive, positive theology; finally, Deleuze's philosophy of life contains a *spiritual power* that expresses a spirituality of life, a way of living that exceeds all possible distinction between theology and philosophy and one that could form the basis of a challenging theology of life.

Notes

Introduction

1 See, for example, DI, p. 262, and Holsinger Sherman, J. (2009), 'No werewolves in theology?'
2 Hardt, M. (1993), *Gilles Deleuze. An Apprenticeship in Philosophy*. Minneapolis: University of Minnesota Press, p. 58.
3 Milbank, J. (2011), 'Stanton Lecture 1. The return of metaphysics in the 21st century': http://www.abc.net.au/religion/articles/2011/01/28/3123584.htm?topic1=home&topic2.
4 Crockett, C. (2011), *Radical Political Theology. Religion and Politics after Liberalism*. New York: Columbia University Press, p. 2.

Chapter 1

1 De Beistegui, M. (2010), *Immanence - Deleuze and Philosophy*. Edinburgh: Edinburgh University Press, p. 5.
2 Goodchild, P. (2001), 'Why philosophy is so compromised with God', in M. Bryden (ed.), *Deleuze and Religion*. London: Routledge, p. 157.
3 Williams, J. (2003), *Gilles Deleuze's Difference and Repetition: A Critical Introduction and Guide*. Edinburgh: Edinburgh University Press, p. 198.
4 Deleuze and Guattari described this process in *What Is Philosophy?*; WP, pp. 44–9.
5 See Thacker, E. (2010), *After Life*. Chicago: The University of Chicago Press, p. 135: 'Unlike Aquinas and Henry, he [Duns Scotus] comes very close to positing univocal being as something "beyond" both creature and Creator'.
6 Ibid., p. 136.
7 Cf. ibid., p. 144: 'The Scotist notion of univocity as *neutral being* is transformed by Spinoza into a notion of univocity as *affirmative becoming*. (. . .) In short, it amounts to an ontological assertion of being as fundamentally generous – being always flows, is always productive and proliferate, is always in excess'.

8 DR, 51: 'Eternal return is the univocity of being, the effective realization of that univocity. In the eternal return, univocal being is not only thought and even affirmed, but effectively realized. Being is said in a single and same sense, but this sense is that of eternal return as the return or repetition of that of which it is said'.
9 Williams, J. (2003), *Gilles Deleuze's Difference and Repetition*, p. 62.
10 See also: LS, p. 178: 'The univocity of Being signifies that Being is Voice that it is said, and that it is said in one and the same "sense" of everything about which it is said'; DR, p. 378: 'A single and same voice for the whole thousand-voiced multiple, a single and same Ocean for all the drops, a single clamour of Being for all beings'; LS, p. 180: '. . . one Being and only for all forms and all times, a single instance for all that exists, a single phantom for all the living, a single voice for every hum of voices and every drop of water in the sea'.
11 Thacker, E. *After Life*, p. 112: 'Its [analogy's] general contours had already been suggested by William of Auvergne, Albert the Great, and Bonaventure, before Aquinas had formalized it in the *Summa*'.
12 Ibid., p. 111.
13 Ibid., p. 112.
14 Ibid., p. 116.
15 Thacker, E., *After Life*, p. 185.
16 Bryant, L. (2008), *Difference and Giveness. Deleuze's Transcendental Empiricism and the Ontology of Immanence*. Evanston: Northwestern University Press, p. 78.
17 Ibid., p. 177.
18 Spinoza, B., *Ethics II*, proposition 42. (From Spinoza, *Ethics* (2000) (ed. and trans. By G.H.R. Parkinson). Oxford: Oxford University Press).
19 Spinoza, B., *Ethics V*, proposition 33.
20 Hardt, M. (1993), *Gilles Deleuze. An Apprenticeship in Philosophy*. Minneapolis, University of Minnesota Press, p. 116.
21 Hallward, P. (2006), *Out of This World. Deleuze and the Philosophy of Creation*. New York: Verso, p. 4.
22 Deleuze refers to Merleau-Ponty, M. (ed.) (1956), *Les philosophes célèbres*. Paris: Mazenod, p. 136.
23 Hardt, M., *Gilles Deleuze*, pp. 63–4. See also EP, 53: 'That theology that is called negative admits that affirmations are able to designate God as cause, subject to rules of immanence which lead from what is nearest to what is farthest from him. but God as substance or essence can be defined only negatively, according to rules of transcendence whereby one denies in their turn names that are farthest from him, then those that are nearest'.
24 See Taylor, C. (2007), *The Secular Age*. Cambridge: The Belknap Press of Harvard University Press.

NOTES

25 Cf. Derrida, J. (1978), *Writing and Difference* (trans. A. Bass). Chicago: Chicago University Press; (1993) *Khôra*. Paris: Galilée; (1994) *Force de loi. Le 'fondement mystique de l'autorité'*. Paris: Galilée; (1995) *On the Name* (trans. T. Dutoit). Stanford: Stanford University Press;
26 De Beistegui, M. (2010), *Immanence – Deleuze and Philosophy*, p. 193.
27 McDaniel, J. (2007), 'Ecotheology and worldreligions', in L. Kearns & C. Keller (eds.), *Ecospirit. Religions and Philosophies for the Earth*. New York: Fordham University Press, p. 29.
28 Higgins, L. (2007), 'Toward a Deleuze-Guattarian micropneumatology of spirit-dust', in ibid., p. 253.
29 Hallward, P., *Out of This World*, p. 6.
30 Higgins, L., 'Toward a Deleuze-Guattarian micropneumatology of spirit-dust', p. 253.
31 Ibid., p. 254.
32 Cf. Latour, B. (2004), *Politics of Nature: How to Bring the Sciences Into Democracy* (trans. Catherine Porter). Cambridge, MA: Harvard University Press.
33 Higgins, L., 'Toward a Deleuze-Guattarian micropneumatology of spirit-dust', p. 259.
34 Deleuze and Guattari would like to 'produce a sort of philosophy of Nature, now that any distinction between nature and artifice is becoming blurred' (see N, p. 155).
35 AO, p. 4: 'We make no distinction between man and nature: the human essence of nature and the natural essence of man become one within nature in the form of production or industry, just as they do within the life of man as a species'. See also Smith, A. P. (2010), 'Believing in this world for the making of gods. Ecology of the virtual and the actual'. *SubStance*, pp. 121, 103–14, 105: 'From the perspective of schizoanalysis, there is no difference in kind between humanity and nature, only a difference of degree'.
36 Ibid., p. 110.

Chapter 2

1 Hardt, M. (1993), *Gilles Deleuze. An Apprenticeship in Philosophy*. Minneapolis: Minnesota University Press, p. 74.
2 Goodchild, P. (2010), 'Philosophy as a way of life. Deleuze on thinking and money'. *SubStance*, 39/1, 24–37, 25.
3 Ibid., p. 26.
4 See Braidotti, R. (1994) *Nomadic Subjects. Embodiment and Sexual Difference in ContemporaryFeminist Theory*. New York: Columbia

University Press; (2001) 'Becoming-woman. Rethinking the positivity of difference', in E. Bronfen and M. Kavka (eds.), *Feminist Consequences*. New York: Columbia University Press, pp. 381–413.

5 See Hardt, M., *Gilles Deleuze*, pp. 119–20: 'I have tried to discover in Deleuze some tools for the constitution of a radical democracy. [. . .] From this perspective, Deleuze can help us develop a dynamic conception of democratic society as open, horizontal, and collective'. See also Hardt, M. and Negri, A. (2004), *Multitude. War and Democracy in the Age of Empire*. New York: the Penguin Press.

6 Cf. LS, pp. 301–21.

7 Hallward, P. (1997), 'Deleuze and the "world without others"'. *Philosophy Today*, 41/4, 530–44, 531: 'A difference which becomes active, very precisely, through the literal extinction of specific differences'.

8 LS, p. 305: 'For all of us the presence of other people is a powerful element of distraction, not only because they constantly break into our activities and interrupt our train of thought, but because the mere possibility of their doing so illumines a world of concerns situated at the edge of our consciousness but capable at any moment of becoming its center'. Deleuze cites Michel Tournier (1967), *Vendredi ou les limbes du Pacifique*. Paris: Gallimard, p. 32; English translation *Friday* (1985) (trans. N. Denny), New York: Pantheon Books, p. 38.

9 LS, p. 313 : 'When we desire Others, are not our desires brought to bear upon this expressed small possible world which the Other wrongly envelops, instead of allowing it to float and fly above the world, developed onto a glorious double?'

10 Hallward, P. (1997), 'Gilles Deleuze and the redemption from interest'. *Radical Philosophy*, 81, 6–21, p. 6.

11 Hallward, P. (2006), *Out of This World. Deleuze and the Philosophy of Creation*, New York: Verso.

12 D, p. 2: 'Becomings belong to geography, they are orientations, directions, entries and exits. There is a woman-becoming which is not the same as women, their past and their future, and it is essential that women enter this becoming to get out of their past and their future, their history. (. . .) To become is never to imitate, nor [sic] to 'do like', nor [sic] to conform to a model, whether it's of justice or of truth. (. . .) The question, "What are you becoming ?" is particularly stupid. For as someone becomes, what he is becoming changes as much as he does himself. Becomings are not phenomena of imitation or assimilation, but of a double capture, of non-parallel evolution, of nuptials between two reigns'.

13 ATP, p. 308: 'What are they all rushing toward? Without a doubt, toward becoming-imperceptible. The imperceptible is the immanent end of becoming, its cosmic formula'. So it is not about becoming-nothing, but rather about becoming-'everything', becoming pure energy.

14 See Braidotti, R. (2001), 'Becoming-woman. Rethinking the positivity of difference', in E. Bronfen & M. Kavka (eds.), *Feminist Consequences*. New York: Columbia University Press, p. 393.
15 Irigaray, L. (1985), *This Sex Which Is Not One*. Ithaca: Cornell University Press, p. 24.
16 See Colebrook, C. (2000), 'Introduction', in I. Buchanan and C. Colebrook (eds.), *Deleuze and Feminist Theory*, p. 14; and Colebrook, C. (2000), 'Chapter 3: The Woman in Process: Deleuze, Kristeva and Feminism', in ibid., pp. 64–85.
17 Irigaray, L., This Sex Which Is Not One, p. 28.
18 Braidotti, R. (1994), *Nomadic Subjects. Embodiment and Sexual Difference in Contemporary Feminist Theory*. New York: Columbia University Press, p. 120: 'Deleuze's "becoming-woman" amalgamates men and women into a new, supposedly beyond gender, sexuality; this is problematic, because it clashes with women's sense of their own historical struggles'.
19 MacCormack, P. (2001), 'Becoming human: Deleuze and Guattari, gender and 3rd rock from the sun'. *Intensities. Journal of cult Media*, 1. http://intensities.org/essays/MacCormack.pdf
20 Flieger, J. A. (2000), 'Becoming-woman. Deleuze, Schreber and molecular identification', in C. Colebrook and I. Buchanan, *Deleuze and Feminist Theory*. Edinburgh: Edinburgh University Press, pp. 38–63, 43.
21 ATP, p. 20: 'Does not the East, Oceania in particular, offer something like a rhizomatic model opposed in every respect to the Western model of the tree? André Haudricourt even sees this as the basis for the opposition between the moralities or philosophies of transcendence dear to the West and the immanent ones of the East: the God who sows and reaps, as opposed to the God who replants and unearths (replanting of offshoots versus sowing of seeds). Transcendence: a specifically European disease'.
22 ATP, p. 20: 'We have lost the rhizome, or the grass. Henry Miller: "China is the weed in the human cabbage patch. (. . .) Eventually the weed gets the upper hand. (. . .) Grass is the only way out. . . . The weed exists only to fill the waste spaces left by cultivated areas. *It grows between*, among other things"'.
23 ATP, p. 309: 'The fish is like the Chinese poet: not imitative or structural, but cosmic (..) They [Chinese poets] retain, extract only the essential lines and movements of nature; they proceed only by continued or superposed "traits", or strokes'.
24 Two important nuances need to be mentioned here, however. First, the preference for the deterritorialization of lines of flight does not necessarily mean that lines of flight always lead to 'more life', more freedom; sometimes, Deleuze and Guattari admit, a line of flight turns against itself and becomes destructive. After all, lines of flight remain an experiment and can therefore become

destructive lines, as was the case, for example, in fascism. See also Hallward, P. (1997), 'Deleuze and the "world without others"'. *Philosophy Today*, 41/4, 530–44. Second, the exclusivity of the preference for deterritorialization needs to be nuanced. In *Anti-Oedipus*, deterritorialization is pictured as something 'good', something that initiates a permanent revolution, whereas reterritorialization seemed to be a bad evolution. In *A Thousand Plateaus*, however, the concept is widened and the process deterritorialization contains a movement of reterritorialization *within* itself. The binary opposition is thus less sharp, deterritorialization lies at the basis of both movements. See also Holland, E. (1991), 'Deterritorializing "deterritorialization". From anti-oedipus to "a thousand plateaus"'. *SubStance* 20/3, 55–65, esp. pp. 58 and 59. See also Higgings, L. (2007), 'Toward a Deleuze–Guattarian micropneumatology of spirit-dust', in L. Kearns & C. Keller, *Ecospirit. Religions and Philosophies for the Earth*. New York: Fordham University Press, pp. 252–63, 257: 'Deleuze–Guattari often describe this stratification process in negative terms – the free, creative motions of molecular particles become oppressed by a falsely unifying logic of organization. At other points in their work, however, they make clear that it is not mere existence of strata that is problematic but only the illusion that *particular* stratified, molar structures are inevitable'.

25 Smith, A. P. (2010), 'Believing in this world for the making of gods. Ecology of the virtual and the actual'. *SubStance* 39/1, 103–14, 103–4.
26 Jantzen, G. (1999), *Becoming Divine. Towards a Feminist Philosophy of Religion*. Bloomington: Indiana University Press, p. 7.
27 Ibid., p. 10.
28 Irigaray, L. (1993), *Sexes and Genealogies*. New York: Columbia University Press, p. 61.
29 Ibid., p. 62.
30 Grosz, E. (1993), 'Irigaray and the divine', in C.W. Maggie Kim, Susan St Ville and Susan Simonaitis (eds.), *Transfigurations: Theology and the French Feminists*. Minneapolis: Fortress Press, p. 208.
31 Ibid., p. 210.
32 Eckhart, Meister (1963), *Deutsche Predigten und Traktate* (ed. J. Quint). München – Vienna: Carl Hanser Verlag, p. 7: '*Wer diese Rede nicht versteht, der bekümmere sein Herz nicht damit. Denn solange der Mensch dieser Wahrheit nicht gleicht, solange wird er diese Rede nicht verstehen*' (my translation into English).
33 Eckhart, Meister (1979), *Sermons and Treatises. Volume I* (trans. and ed. E. Walshe). Longmead: Element Books, p. 117.
34 Decorte, J. (1992), Waarheid als weg. Beknopte geschiedenis van de middeleeuwse wijsbegeerte. Kapellen: Pelckmans, p. 260.

35 McGinn, B. (2001), *The Mystical Thought of Meister Eckhart. The Man From Whom God Hid Nothing*. New York: The Crossroad Publishing Company, p. 45. McGinn refers to Langer, O. (1987) 'Meister Eckharts Lehre vom Seelengrund', in M. Schmidt and D. R. Bauer (eds.), *Grundfragen christliche Mystik*. Stuttgart/Bad Cannstatt: frommann-holzboog, pp. 173–91.
36 McGinn, B., The Mystical Thought of Meister Eckhart, p. 48.
37 Eckhart, Meister (1979), *Sermons & Treatises. Volume II* (trans. and ed. M. Walshe). Longmead: Element Books, p. 98.
38 McGinn, B., *The Mystical Thought of Meister Eckhart. The Man from Whom God Hid Nothing*.
39 Eckhart, *Sermons and Treatises. Volume I*, p. 118.
40 Eckhart, *Sermons and Treatises. Volume II*, pp. 85–6 (my italics).
41 McGinn, B., *The Mystical Thought of Meister Eckhart*, p. 71ff.
42 Eckhart, *Sermons and Treatises. Volume II*, p. 87.
43 Eckhart, *Sermons and Treatises. Volume II*, pp. 98–9.
44 To the extent that I could also have discussed someone like Nicolas of Cusa (1401–64), whom Deleuze sometimes mentioned in his works, and who is, perhaps, more obviously a univocal thinker.
45 WP, p. 45: 'Putting their work and sometimes their lives at risk, all philosophers must prove that the dose of immanence they inject into world and mind does not compromise the transcendence of a God to which immanence must be attributed only secondarily (Nicholas of Cusa, Eckhart, Bruno)'.
46 However, insight and belief are both present in Deleuze's thought, and difficult to discern from each other, see WP, 75: 'It may be that believing in this world, in this life, becomes our most difficult task. . .'. But the Deleuzian belief, of course, is still not the same as the expression of an act of faith, as a confession.
47 Batchelor, S. (1997), *Buddhism Without Beliefs*. New York: Riverhead Books, p. 62.
48 Ibid., p. 70.
49 Ibid., p. 18.
50 Two important objections could be made to a connection of Deleuze with Buddhism. First, we know Buddhism as a world view that wants to rule out all desires, whereas Deleuze gives the impression to liberate desire from any form of oppression. And this is true. But eventually, Buddhist and Deleuze's aspirations turn out to be the same: Deleuze wants to 'restore' desire as an 'objective' stream that is not bound to actual needs of a subject (desire is never *my* desire), and Buddhism strives for the same thing: not the desire has disappeared but the attachment of the subject to its desires; see Gowans, C. W. (2003), *Philosophy of the Buddha*. London & New York: Routlegde, p. 37. Second, one could contrast the 'emptiness' to which everything is reducible in Buddhism (*Sunyata*) with

Deleuze's fullness of being – but in that case, one has not understood the Buddhist emptiness properly: 'This is emptiness: not a cosmic vacuum but the unborn, undying, infinitely creative dimension of life. It is known as the womb of awakening'; it is the clearing in the still center of becoming', Batchelor, S., *Buddhism without Beliefs*, p. 9.
51 Lawlor, L. (2006), *The Implications of Immanence: Towards a New Concept of Life*. New York: Fordham University Press, p. 144.
52 Ibid.
53 Eckhart, Meister (1963), *Deutsche Predigten und Traktate* (ed. J. Quint), p. 286 (my translation into English).

Chapter 3

1 DR, p. 69: 'Difference is behind everything, but behind difference, there is nothing.'
2 Bergson, H. (1924), *Creative Evolution* (trans. Arthur Mitchell). New York: Henry Holt and Company, p. 248.
3 Hardt, M. (1993), *Gilles Deleuze. An Apprenticeship in Philosophy*. Minneapolis: University of Minnesota Press, p. 17. This is different from the process of 'realization' with the dualism 'potentiality – reality'. The process of realization is determined by determination, by limiting the possibilities: it is thus a negative process. See B, 97: 'Realization involves a limitation by which some possibles are supposed to be repulsed or thwarted, while others "pass" into the real. The virtual, on the other hand, does not have to be realized, but rather actualized ; and the rules of actualization are not those of resemblance and limitation, but those of difference or divergence and of creation'.
4 Hallward, P. (2006), *Out of This World. Deleuze and the Philosophy of Creation*. London: Verso, p. 3.
5 Robinson, K. (2010), 'Back to life: Deleuze, Whitehead and process'. *Deleuze Studies* 4, 120–33, p. 120.
6 Williams, J. (2010), 'Immanence and transcendence as inseparable processes: On the relevance of arguments from Whitehead to Deleuze interpretation'. *Deleuze Studies* 4, 94–106.
7 Cf. C. Crockett (2011), *Radical Political Theology*. New York: Columbia University Press, p. 10.
8 Cf. Shaviro, S. (2009), *Without Criteria. Kant, Whitehead, Deleuze and Aesthetics*. Cambridge, MA: The MIT Press, p. 103.
9 Whitehead, A. N. (1978), *Process and Reality*. New York: The Free Press, p. 7: 'In monistic philosophies, Spinoza's or absolute idealism, this ultimate is God, who is also equivalently termed "The

Absolute". In such monistic schemes, the ultimate is illegitimately allowed a final, "eminent" reality, beyond that ascribed to any of its accidents.'
10 Williams, J., 'Immanence and transcendence as inseparable processes', p. 95.
11 Whitehead, A. N., *Process and Reality*, p. 346: 'The vicious separation of the flux from the permanence leads to the concept of an entirely static God, with eminent reality, in relation to an entirely fluent world, with deficient reality.'
12 Whitehead, A. N., *Process and Reality*, p. 348.
13 Williams, J., 'Immanence and transcendence as inseparable processes', p. 96.
14 Whitehead, A. N., *Process and Reality*, p. 172.
15 Shaviro, S., *Without Criteria*, p. 112
16 Ibid., p. 128.
17 Ibid., pp. 128–9.
18 LS, p. 176 : 'Sense expressed as an event is of an entirely different nature (. . .). It is a pure sign whose coherence excludes merely, and yet supremely, the coherence of the self, world, and God.'
19 Whitehead, A. N., *Process and Reality*, p. 164.
20 Whitehead, A. N. (1967), *Science and the Modern World*. New York: The Free Press, p. 178. See also Clark, T. (2002), 'A Whiteheadian chaosmos? Process philosophy from a Deleuzean perspective,' in C. Keller and A. Daniell, *Process and Difference*. New York: SUNY, pp. 191–208, in which he argues that Whitehead's universe is still predictable to a certain extent, in opposition to Deleuze's 'chaosmos'.
21 Whitehead, A. N. (1967) *Adventures of Ideas*, New York: The Free Press, p. 115.
22 Unless, as Deleuze describes in *The Fold*, his book on Leibniz, in a kind of 'new harmony' in which several divergent series can be traced within the same chaosmos (F, p. 92).
23 See also De Bolle, L. (2009), 'Bergson,' in E. Romein, M. Schuilenburg and S. van Tuinen (eds.), *Deleuze Compendium*. Amsterdam: Boom, pp. 81–96, 89.
24 De Bolle, L., 'Bergson', p. 95.
25 Deleuze, G. (1999), Nietzsche. Paris: PUF, pp. 37–8: '*Le secret de Nietzsche, c'est que l'éternel Retour est sélectif. (. . .) Seule revient l'affirmation, seul revient ce qui peut être affirmé, seule la joie retourne*'. (My translation into English.)
26 Ibid., p. 40
27 Ibid., p. 40.
28 Ibid., p. 38: '*L'éternel Retour doit être comparé à une roué; mais le mouvement de la rolué est doué d'un pouvoir centrifuge, qui chasse tout le négative. Parce que l'Être s'affirme du devenir, il expulse de soi tout ce qui contredit l'affirmation, toutes les formes du nihilisme

et de la réaction: mauvaise conscience, ressentiment. . . , on ne les verra qu'une fois'. (My translation into English.)

29 Beinert, W. and Schüssler Fiorenza, F. (eds.) (1995), *Handbook of Catholic Theology*, New York: Crossroad, pp. 133–53. See also Gilkey, L. B. (1959), *Maker of Heaven and Earth: A Study of the Christian Doctrine of Creation.* Garden City (NJ): Doubleday, p. 193: 'The total structure of man's being as creature made out of nothing roots his life beyond himself in the transcendent source of his existence, in God his Creator and preserver.'

30 Cf. Prigogine, I. and Stengers, I. (1984), *Order Out of Chaos. Man's New Dialogue with Nature.* London: Heinemann, in which the authors demonstrate how systems automatically evolve towards more order and complexity.

31 Keller, C. (2002), *The Face of the Deep: A theology of Becoming.* London: Routledge, p. xvi.

32 Ibid., p. 5; Keller refers to Said, E. (1975), *Beginnings. Intention and Method.* New York: Basic Books.

33 Said, E. (1975), *Beginnings. Intention and Method*, p. 373.

34 Keller, C., *The Face of the Deep*, p. 158.

35 Hardt, M. (1993), *Gilles Deleuze. An Apprenticeship in Philosophy.* Minneapolis: University of Minnesota Press, p. xiii.

36 Keller, C., *The Face of the Deep*, pp. 15–16.

37 Ibid., p. 17.

38 Ibid., p. 19.

39 Westhelle, V. (1990), 'Creation motifs in the search for a vital space: a Latin American perspective,' in S. B. Thistlethwaite and M. P. Engel (eds.), *Lift Every Voice. Constructing Christian Theologies from the Underside.* San Franscisco: Harper and Row, pp. 128–40.

40 Ibid., p. 130.

41 Ibid., p. 131.

42 Bauman, W. A. (2007), 'Creatio ex nihilo, terra nullius, and the erasure of presence,' in L. Kearns and C. Keller (eds.) *Ecospirit. Religions and Philosophies for the Earth.* New York: Fordham University Press, pp. 353–72, 355.

43 Keller, C., *The Face of the Deep*, p. xviii.

44 Ibid., p. 168.

45 Ibid., p. 168. Keller refers to DR, 305.

46 Ibid., p. 171.

47 Ibid., p. 12.

48 Ibid., p. 173.

49 Ibid., p. 173. Keller refers to an unpublished manuscript by Lynn Bechtel, 'Genesis 1.1-2.4a revisited: the perpetuation of what is', p. 6.

50 Cf. Robinson, K., 'Back to life', p. 131, n.5 [On the basic structure of the event]: 'On the one hand a state of affairs that relates to actualized bodies and individuals and, on the other, an incorporeal reserve

of infinite becoming and virtual movement. Treating this structure as a simple hierarchical dualism has been used to give a distorted image of Deleuze's thought. I suggest that a better image is the 'between-two' or 'fourfold' where each component is internal to and completed by the other. In terms of the Deleuze and Whitehead event extension, intension, prehension and ingression each have a virtual/actual side and the process of conversion between them is carried out by different modes of creativity.'
51 Keller, C. (2007), 'Complicities: folding the event in Whitehead and Deleuze', http://users.drew.edu/ckeller/essays-download.html, p. 3
52 Ibid., p. 3.
53 Ibid., p. 5.
54 Robinson, K., 'Back to life', pp. 124–5.
55 Isherwood, L. and Bellchambers, E. (2010), 'Introduction', in L. Isherwood and E. Bellchambers (eds.), *Through Us, With Us, In Us: Relational Theologies in the Twenty-First Century*. London: SCM Press, p. 2.
56 Heyward, C. (2010), 'Breaking points: shaping a relational theology, in L. Isherwood and E. Bellchambers, *Through Us, With Us, In Us: Relational Theologies in the Twenty-First Century*, p. 10.
57 Keller, C., 'Complicities', p. 7.
58 Isherwood, L. and Bellchambers E., 'Introduction', p. 2.
59 Higgins, L. (2007), 'Toward a Deleuze–Guattarian micropneumatology of spirit-dust', in L. Kearns and C. Keller, *Ecospirit*. New York: Fordham University Press, pp. 252–63, 257–8.
60 Heyward, C., 'Breaking points', p. 13.
61 Cf. Smith, A. P. (2010), 'Believing in this world for the making of Gods: ecology of the virtual and the actual'. *Substance* 39/1, 103–14, 108.
62 ATP, 278: 'Theology is very strict on the following point: there are no werewolves, human beings cannot become animal. That is because there is no transformation of essential forms; they are inalienable and only entertain relations of analogy'. See also J. Holsinger Sherman (2009), 'No werewolves in theology? Transcendence, immanence and becoming-divine in Gilles Deleuze'. *Modern Theology* 25/1, 1–20.
63 Higgins, L. (2010), 'A Logos without organs: Cosmologies of transformation in Origen and Deleuze–Guattari'. *SubStance* 39/1, 141–53.

Chapter 4

1 Cf. Buchanan, I. and Parr, A. (2006), 'Introduction', in I. Buchanan and A. Parr (eds.), *Deleuze and the Contemporary World*. Edinburgh: Edinburgh University Press, pp. 1–20, 1.
2 Patton, P. (2000), Deleuze and the Political. London: Routledge, pp. 83–5.

3 Bogue, R. (2007), *Deleuze's Way. Essays in Transverse Ethics and Aesthetics*. Aldershot: Ashgate, p. 3.
4 Goodchild, P. (2010), 'Philosophy as a way of life: Deleuze on thinking and money'. *SubStance* 39/1, 24–37, 28.
5 Buchanan, I. (2008), 'Power, theory and praxis', in I. Buchanan and N. Thoburn, *Deleuze and the Political*. Edinburgh: Edinburgh University Press, pp. 13–34, 14.
6 Cf. Surin, K. (2009), *Freedom Not Yet. Liberation and the Next World Order*. Durham: Duke University Press, p. 242.
7 Goodchild, P., 'Philosophy as a way of life', pp. 28–9.
8 Ibid., p. 29.
9 Surin, K., *Freedom Not Yet*, p. 261.
10 Thoburn, N. (2006), 'Vacuoles of noncommunication: Minor politics, communist style and the multitude', in I. Buchanan and A. Parr (eds.), *Deleuze and the Contemporary World*, pp. 42–56, 53: 'Minor politics is less about the formation of a political subject and the development of universal tools of theory in a language 'that everybody can understand' – an apparently laudable aim that in practice can leave a text shorn of its productive relation with material environments – than about the generation of intimate, engaged and particular problematics in diffuse foci of creation, what Deleuze might call "vacuoles of noncommunication". One hopes that these intensify, multiply and consolidate at a popular level, but a widespread social formation will not occur through an act of popular recognition or inclusion in a set of political concepts and narratives'.
11 Klein, N. (2001), 'Reclaiming the Commons'. *New Left Review* 9, 81–9, 89.
12 Buchanan, I. and Parr, A., 'Introduction', p. 11.
13 Hertz, N. (2004), *I.O.U. The Debt Thread and Why We Must Defuse It*. London: Fourth Estate.
14 Surin, K., *Freedom Not Yet*, p. 261.
15 Buchanan, I. and Parr, A., 'Introduction', p. 10.
16 See Sölle, D. (2001), *The Silent Cry: Mysticism and Resistance* (trans. B. & M. Rumscheidt). Minneapolis: Fortress.
17 Cf. J. Ratzinger, Relación sobre la situación actual de la fe y la teología, in Fe y teologiá en America Itina (Santa Fe de Bogota, Colombia: CELAM, 1997), p. 14, quoted in Petrella, I. (2006), *The Future of Liberation Theology. An Argument and Manifesto*. London: SCM Press, p. 25: 'The fall of the European governmental systems based on Marxism turned out to be a kind of twilight of the gods for that theology'.
18 Petrella, I., *The Future of Liberation Theology*, pp. 12–13.
19 Robbins, J. W. (2006), 'Terror and the postmodern condition: toward a radical political theology', in C. Crockett (ed.), *Religion and Violence in a Secular World: Toward a New Political Theology*. Charlottesville: University of Virginia Press, p. 10.

20 Althaus-Reid, M. (2000), *Indecent Theology. Theological Perversions in Sex, Gender and Politics*. London: Routledge, pp. 171–2.
21 Cf. Petrella, I., *The Future of Liberation Theology*, pp. 10, 121.
22 Ibid., p. 37.
23 L. Boff and C. Boff (1987), *Introducing Liberation Theology* (transl. Paul Burns). Maryknoll: Orbis Books, pp. 28–32.
24 De Certeau, M. (1984), *The Practice of Everyday Life* (trans. S. Randall). Berkeley: University of California Press, pp. 35–6.
25 Ibid., p. 37.
26 Cf. Petrella, I., *The Future of Liberation Theology*, p. 6: 'Resistance is "not an ideological declaration of principles nor [sic] can be reduced to a political program. Resistance occurs in everyday life, it is found in the cyclical rituals of community life"'. Petrella refers to Trigo, P. (1993), 'El future de la teología de la liberación', in J. Comblin, J. Faus and J. Sobrino (eds.), *Cambio Social y Pensamiento Cristiano en América Latina*. Madrid: Editorial Trotta, p. 312. Trigo broadens the strictly macropolitical scope of traditional liberation theology.
27 See Justaert, K. (2010), 'Liberation theology: Deleuze and Althaus-Reid'. *SubStance* 39/1, 154–64.
28 Althaus-Reid, M. (2004), *From Feminist Theology to Indecent Theology*. London: SCM Press, p. 52.
29 Ibid., p. 48.
30 Bell, D. M. (2001), *Liberation Theology after the End of History. The Refusal to Cease Suffering*. London: Routledge, p. 86.
31 Ibid., p. 98.
32 Ibid., p. 144.
33 Ibid., p. 72.
34 Ibid., p. 74.
35 Petrella, I., *The Future of Liberation Theology*, p. 130.
36 See Milbank, J. (2006), *Theology and Social Theory: Beyond Secular Reason*. Oxford: Blackwell.
37 Petrella, I., *The Future of Liberation Theology*, p. 130.
38 See also Justaert, K., 'Liberation theology: Deleuze and Althaus-Reid', pp. 159–60.
39 Macgregor Wise, J. (2004), 'Assemblage', in C.J. Stivale (ed.), *Gilles Deleuze: Key Concepts*. Chesham, England: Acumen, p. 80.

Conclusion

1 See Segundo, J. L. (1976), *Liberation of Theology*. Maryknoll: Orbis Books.
2 See Van Bladel, L. (1980), *Christelijk geloof en maatschappijkritiek*. Antwerpen/Amsterdam: Uitgeverij De Nederlandsche Boekhandel, pp. 11–27.

Bibliography

Althaus-Reid, M. (2000), *Indecent Theology. Theological Perversions in Sex, Gender and Politics*. London: Routledge.
—(2004), *From Feminist Theology to Indecent Theology*. London: SCM Press.
Batchelor, S. (1997), *Buddhism Without Beliefs*. New York: Riverhead Books.
Bauman, W. A. (2007), 'Creatio ex nihilo, terra nullius, and the erasure of presence', in L. Kearns and C. Keller (eds), *Ecospirit. Religions and Philosophies for the Earth*. New York: Fordham University Press, 353–72.
Beinert, W. and Schüssler Fiorenza, F. (eds) (2000), *Handbook of Catholic Theology*. New York: The Crossroad Publishing Company.
Bell, D. M. (2001), *Liberation Theology After the End of History. The Refusal to Cease Suffering*. London: Routledge.
Bergson, H. (1924), *Creative Evolution* (trans. A. Mitchell). New York: Henry Holt and Company.
Boff, L. and Boff, C. (1987), *Introducing Liberation Theology* (trans. P. Burns). Maryknoll, NY: Orbis Books.
Bogue, R. (2007), *Deleuze's Way. Essays in Transverse Ethics and Aesthetics*. Aldershot: Ashgate.
Braidotti, R. (1994), *Nomadic Subjects. Embodiment and Sexual Difference in Contemporary Feminist Theory*. New York: Columbia University Press.
—(2001), 'Becoming-Woman. Rethinking the positivity of difference', in E. Bronfen and M. Kavka (eds), *Feminist Consequences*. New York: Columbia University Press, 381–413.
Buchanan, I. (2008), 'Power, theory and praxis', in I. Buchanan and N. Thoburn (eds), *Deleuze and the Political*. Edinburgh: Edinburgh University Press, 13–34.
Buchanan, I. and Colebrook, C. (eds) (2000), *Deleuze and Feminist Theory*. Edinburgh: Edinburgh University Press.
Buchanan, I. and Parr, A. (2006), 'Introduction', in I. Buchanan and A. Parr (eds), *Deleuze and the Contemporary World*. Edinburgh: Edinburgh University Press, 1–20.

Clark, T. (2002), 'A Whiteheadianchaosmos? Process philosophy from a Deleuzean perspective', in C. Keller and A. Daniell (eds), *Process and Difference*. New York: SUNY, 191–208.
Crockett, C. (2011), *Radical Political Theology. Religion and Politics After Liberalism*. New York: Columbia University Press.
De Certeau, M. (1984), *The Practice of Everyday Life* (trans. S. Randall). Berkeley, CA: University of California Press.
Decorte, J. (1992), *Waarheid als weg. Beknopte geschiedenis van de middeleeuwse wijsbegeerte*. Kapellen: Pelckmans.
Deleuze, G. (1988), *Spinoza: Practical Philosophy* (trans. R. Hurley). San Francisco, CA: City Light Books.
—(1989), *Cinema 2. The Time-Image* (trans. H. Tomlinson and R. Galeta). London: The Athlone Press.
—(1990), *The Logic of Sense* (trans. M. Lester). New York: Columbia University Press.
—(1991), *Bergsonism* (trans. H. Tomlinson and B. Habberjam). New York: Zone Books.
—(1992), *Expressionism in Philosophy: Spinoza* (trans. M. Joughin). New York: Zone Books.
—(1995), *Negotiations 1972–90* (trans. M. Joughin). New York: Columbia University Press.
—(1999), *Nietzsche*. Paris: PUF.
—(2004), *Desert Islands and Other Texts 1953–74* (trans. M. Taormina). Los Angeles, CA: Semiotext(e).
—(2004), *Difference and Repetition* (trans. P. Patton). London: Continuum.
—(2006), *The Fold* (trans. T. Conley). London: Continuum.
—(2006), *Nietzsche and Philosophy* (trans. H. Tomlinson). New York: Columbia University Press.
—(2007), *Two Regimes of Madness. Texts and Interviews 1975–95* (trans. A. Hodges and M. Taormina). Los Angeles, CA: Semiotext(e).
Deleuze, G. and Guattari, F. (1986), *Kafka. Toward a Minor Literature* (trans. D. Polan). Minneapolis, MN: University of Minnesota Press.
—(1994), *What Is Philosophy?* (trans. H. Tomlinson and G. Burchell). New York: Columbia University Press.
—(2004a), *A Thousand Plateaus. Capitalism and Schizophrenia* (trans. B. Massumi). London: Continuum.
—(2004b), *Anti-Oedipus. Capitalism and Schizophrenia* (trans. R. Hurley, M. Seemand H. R. Lane). London: Continuum.
Deleuze, G. and Parnet, C. (2006), *Dialogues II* (trans. H. Tomlinson and B. Habberjam). London: Continuum.
Eckhart, M. (1936), *Die Deutschen und Lateinischen Werke Band III*. Stuttgart – Berlin: Verlag von B. Kohlhammer.
—(1963), *Deutsche Predigten und Traktate* (ed. J. Quint). München – Vienna: Carl Hanser Verlag.

—(1979), *Sermons and Treatises*. Volume I & II (trans. and ed. M. Walshe). Longmead: Element Books.
Flieger, J. A. (2000), 'Becoming-woman. Deleuze, Schreber and molecular identification', in C. Colebrook and I. Buchanan (eds), *Deleuze and Feminist Theory*. Edinburgh: Edinburgh University Press, 38–63.
Gilkey, L. B. (1959), *Maker of Heaven and Earth: A Study of the Christian Doctrine of Creation*. Garden City, NJ: Doubleday.
Goodchild, P. (2010a), 'Philosophy as a way of life: Deleuze on thinking and money'. *SubStance*, 39(1), 24–37.
—(2010b), 'Philosophy as a way of life:Deleuze on thinking and money'. *SubStance*, 121, 24–37.
Gowans, C. W. (2003), *Philosophy of the Buddha*. London and New York: Routlegde.
Grosz, E. (1993), 'Irigaray and the divine', in C. W. Maggie Kim, S. St Ville and S. Simonaitis (eds), *Transfigurations: Theology and the French Feminists*. Minneapolis, MN: Fortress Press.
Hallward, P. (1997a), 'Deleuze and the "world without others" '. *Philosophy Today*, 41(4), 530–44.
—(1997b), 'Gilles Deleuze and the redemption from interest'. *Radical Philosophy*, 81, 6–21.
—(2006), *Out of This World. Deleuze and the Philosophy of Creation*. London: Verso.
Hardt, M. (1993), *Gilles Deleuze. An Apprenticeship in Philosophy*. Minneapolis, MN: University of Minnesota Press.
Hardt, M. and Negri, A. (2004), *Multitude. War and Democracy in the Age of Empire*. New York: The Penguin Press.
Hertz, N. (2004), *I.O.U. The Debt Thread and Why We Must Defuse It*. London: Fourth Estate Ltd.
Higgins, L. (2007), 'Toward a Deleuze-Guattarian micropneumatology of spirit-dust', in L. Kearns and C. Keller (eds), *Ecospirit. Religions and Philosophies for the Earth*. New York: Fordham University Press, 252–63.
—(2010), 'A Logos without organs: Cosmologies of transformation in Origen and Deleuze-Guattari'. *SubStance*, 39(1), 141–53.
Holland, E. (1991), 'Deterritorializing "deterritorialisation". From "Anti-Oedipus" to "A Thousand Plateaus"'. *SubStance*, 20(3), 55–65.
Irigaray, L. (1985), *This Sex Which Is Not One*. Ithaca, NY: Cornell University Press.
—(1993), *Sexes and Genealogies*. New York: Columbia University Press.
Isherwood, L. and Bellchambers, E. (eds) (2010), *Through Us, With Us, In Us: Relational Theologies in the Twenty-First Century*. London: SCM Press.
Jantzen, G. (1999), *Becoming Divine. Towards a Feminist Philosophy of Religion*. Bloomington, IN: Indiana University Press.
Justaert, K. (2010), 'Liberation theology: Deleuze and Althaus-Reid'. *SubStance*, 39(1), 154–64.

Keller, C. (2002), *The Face of the Deep: A Theology of Becoming*. London: Routledge.
—(2007), 'Complicities: Folding the event in Whitehead and Deleuze', http://users.drew.edu/ckeller/essays-download.html.
Klein, N. (2001), 'Reclaiming the commons'. *New Left Review*, 9, 81–9.
Langer, O. (1987), 'Meister Eckharts Lehre vom Seelengrund', in M. Schmidt and D. R. Bauer (eds), *Grundfragen christliche Mystik*. Stuttgart-Bad Cannstatt: Frommann-Holzboog, 173–91.
Lawlor, L. (2006), *The Implications of Immanence: Towards a New Concept of Life*. New York: Fordham University Press.
Levinas, E. (1997), *Difficult Freedom. Essays on Judaism* (trans. S. Hand). Baltimore, MD: John Hopkins University Press.
MacCormack, P. (2001), 'Becoming human: Deleuze and Guattari, gender and 3rd rock from the sun'. *Intensities. Journal of Cult Media*, 1, http://intensities.org/essays/MacCormack.pdf.
Macgregor Wise, J. (2004), 'Assemblage', in C. J. Stivale (ed.), *Gilles Deleuze: Key Concepts*. Chesham, England: Acumen.
McGinn, B. (2001), *The Mystical Thought of Meister Eckhart. The Man from Whom God Hid Nothing*. New York: The Crossroad Publishing Company.
Milbank, J. (2006), *Theology and Social Theory: Beyond Secular Reason*. Oxford: Blackwell.
—(2011), 'Stanton Lecture 1. The return of metaphysics in the 21st century', http://www.abc.net.au/religion/articles/2011/01/28/3123584.htm?topic1=home&topic2.
Nijssens, K. (2007), *Spinoza en het problem van de uitdrukking. Deleuzeslezing van Spinoza*. Leuven (unpublished thesis).
Patton, P. (2000), *Deleuze and the Political*. London: Routledge.
Petrella, I. (2006), *TheFuture of Liberation Theology. An Argument and Manifesto*. London: SCM Press.
Prigogine, I. and Stengers, I. (1984), *Order Out of Chaos. Man's New Dialogue with Nature*. London: Heinemann.
Robbins, J. W. (2006), 'Terror and the postmodern condition: Toward a radical political theology', in C. Crockett (ed.), *Religion and Violence in a Secular World: Toward a New Political Theology*. Charlottesville, VA: University of Virginia Press.
Robinson, K. (2010), 'Back to life: Deleuze, Whitehead and process'. *Deleuze Studies*, 4, 120–33.
Romein, E. (2009) Schuilenburg, M. and van Tuinen, S. (eds), *Deleuze Compendium*. Amsterdam: Boom.
Said, E. (1975), *Beginnings. Intention and Method*. New York: Basic Books.
Segundo, J. L. (1976), *Liberation of Theology*. Maryknoll, NY: Orbis Books.

Shaviro, S. (2009), *Without Criteria. Kant, Whitehead, Deleuze and Aesthetics*. Cambridge, MA: The MIT Press.
Sherman, J. H. (2009), 'No werewolves in theology? Transcendence, immanence and becoming-divine in Gilles Deleuze'. *Modern Theology*, 25(1), 1–20.
Silesius, Angelus. (1952), *Sämtliche poetische Werke in drei Bänden. Band 3*, München: Hanser, p. 203.
Smith, A. P. (2010), 'Believing in this world for the making of gods. Ecology of the virtual and the actual'. *SubStance*, 39(1), 103–14.
Sölle, D. (2001), *The Silent Cry: Mysticism and Resistance* (trans. B. Rumscheidt and M. Rumscheidt). Minneapolis, MN: FortressPress.
Surin, K. (2009), *Freedom Not Yet. Liberation and the Next World Order*. Durham, NC: Duke University Press.
Thoburn, N. (2006), 'Vacuoles of noncommunication: Minor politics, communist style and the multitude', in I. Buchanan and A. Parr (eds), *Deleuze and the Contemporary World*, Edinburgh: Edinburgh University Press, 42–56.
Trigo, P. (1993), 'El futura de la teología de la liberación', in J. Comblin, J. Fausand J. Sobrino (eds), *Cambio Social y Pensamiento Cristiano en América Latina*. Madrid: Editorial Trotta.
Van Bladel, L. (1980), *Christelijkgeloof en maatschappijkritiek*. Antwerpen/Amsterdam: Uitgeverij De NederlandscheBoekhandel.
Westhelle, V. (1990), 'Creation motifs in the search for a vital space: A Latin American perspective', in S. B. Thistlethwaite and M. P. Engel (eds), *Lift Every Voice. Constructing Christian Theologies from the Underside*. San Franscisco, CA: Harper and Row, 128–40.
Whitehead, A. N. (1967a), *Adventures of Ideas*. New York: The Free Press, 115.
—(1967b), *Science and the Modern World*. New York: The Free Press.
—(1978), *Process and Reality*. New York: The Free Press.
Williams, J. (2010), 'Immanence and transcendence as inseparable processes: On the relevance of arguments from Whitehead to Deleuze interpretation'. *Deleuze Studies*, 4, 94–106.

Index

actual (the) 14–15, 28, 36, 45, 62, 64, 68, 74–80, 82, 92–3
Althaus-Reid, Marcella 122, 125
anti-production 108–9, 116
Aquinas, Thomas 3, 12, 20–2, 31, 98
Aristotle 3, 20
Augustine 126
axiomatic 104, 106–7, 109–10, 112, 114–15, 117, 122, 133

Bach, Johann Sebastian 82
Bacon, Francis 10
Badiou, Alain 93
Bechtel, Lynn 93
becoming-Christ 62, 125–6
becoming-divine 59
becoming-imperceptible 48–9, 54–6, 62, 67, 76, 119
becoming-woman 48–54
Bell, Daniel 126–8
Bergson, Henri 1, 5, 19, 37, 47, 69, 72–3, 82
Bible 90–1, 93, 103, 120, 124, 126
Bogue, Ronald 106
Braidotti, Rosi 42, 52
Bruno, Giordano 16, 78
Bryant, Levi 25, 27
Buchanan, Ian 115
Buddhism/Zen 61, 66–7

capitalism 102, 104, 107–18, 120–9, 132
Catholicism 3, 83
chaos/chaosmos 79–80, 87–94, 98
China/Chinese 28, 54–6, 59, 67

counter-actualization 62, 75–6
creatio ex nihilo 73, 86–7, 89, 91
Cusa, Nicolas of 78

Darwin, Charles 87
De Beistegui, Miguel 11, 34
De Certeau, Michel 125
debt 108–9, 116
Derrida, Jacques 33, 43, 92
Descartes 16, 23
deterritorialization 11, 14, 50, 54–8, 75–6, 104, 107–17, 125, 128–9
Dickens, Charles 25
disjunctive synthesis 19, 79–80, 97
dualism 4, 8, 13–14, 31, 33–4, 40, 45, 49–50, 74, 121, 132
Duns Scotus 12, 18, 22–3

Eckhart (Meister) 16, 39, 41, 59–66, 116
ecotheology 34–7, 132
Elohim 90, 92–3
emanation 64, 94
Eternal return 18, 72, 83–5
Eucharist 83–4

feminism 8, 34, 42, 49–52, 59–60, 88, 120, 132
Flieger, Jerry 53

Goodchild, Philip 13, 40–1, 106, 113
Grosz, Elisabeth 60
Grunt (ground) 62–4

INDEX

Hallward, Peter 30, 42, 45, 75
Hardt, Michael 39, 42, 89
Hegel, Georg-Wilhelm Friedrich 19, 73, 98
Hertz, Noreena 109, 115
Higgins, Luke 35
Hume, David 5
Husserl, Edmund 16

impersonal 2, 17, 24–5, 27, 30, 32, 41, 51, 67, 73, 84, 113–14, 127, 132
Irigaray, Luce 50–1, 59

Jantzen, Grace 59
Jesus Christ 1, 3, 29, 33, 83–6, 98–100, 103, 120, 125–30

Kafka, Franz 10
Kant, Immanuel 16
Keller, Catherine 88–95
Klein, Naomi 115

Lacan, Jacques 59
Latour, Bruno 36
Lawlor, Leonard 68
Leibniz, Gottfried Wilhelm 96
Levinas, Emmanuel 101

MacCormack, Patricia 52
Marx, Karl 108, 112, 120, 133
Marxism 102, 112, 120
McFague, Sally 35
McGinn, Bernard 63–4
mediation 9, 45, 84, 120, 123, 128, 132
Merleau-Ponty, Maurice 30
micropolitics 52, 54, 104, 114–15, 117
Milbank, John 8, 128
minority 48–50, 53–4, 114, 117–18, 124, 126
molar 47, 52, 57–8, 115,
molecular 47–8, 50, 52–5, 96–8, 104, 114–15, 122, 129

negative theology 30–1, 89
Neo-Platonism 16, 35, 64–5
Nietzsche, Friedrich 1, 5, 18, 46–7, 72, 83, 85, 89
nothingness 63

oppression 107, 120–23, 130, 133
option for the poor, the 120, 123, 125
orthopraxis 120, 123, 125

pantheism 6, 18, 21, 60
Parr, Adrian 115
patriarchal 89–90, 122, 125–6
Patton, Paul 103
Paul (apostle) 44, 64
Péguy, Charles 83
Petrella, Ivan 123, 128
plane of immanence 5, 11–12, 14–18, 26–7, 29–30, 32, 36, 41, 45, 47, 53, 55, 63–4, 78–80, 92, 105, 107–8, 117
Proust, Marcel 82
psychoanalysis 27, 51, 81, 102, 104, 111
pure past 82, 98, 100

queer theology 121, 125, 132

radical orthodoxy 120, 128
relational theology 96–8
repetition 82–4, 98–100
resistance 45, 48, 52, 113, 119–21, 125, 129–30, 133
reterritorialization 57–8, 109, 116, 129
rhizome 55, 67, 72, 78, 80–2, 88, 95–100, 114
Robinson, Keith 76, 93

Said, Edward 88
salvation 5, 11, 17, 42, 45–8, 51, 57–8
Sartre, Jean-Paul 17

INDEX

schizoanalysis 104, 111, 114
schizophrenia 110, 112, 117
Segundo, Juan Luis 131
sexuality 51–2, 88, 121–2, 126
Shaviro, Steven 78–9
Silesius, Angelus 46
sin 121–2
singular 25, 35, 42–3, 57, 84
Smith, Antony Paul 36, 58
Sölle, Dorothee 119
Spinoza, Baruch 1, 5–6, 10, 16–32, 28–31, 40–1, 44–5, 71, 77, 101–2
subjectivity 2, 24–6, 40–1, 45, 51–3, 55, 59, 63, 68, 106, 113, 117, 124, 133
Surin, Kenneth 114, 117

Tauler, Johannes 61
Taylor, Charles 33
tehom 91–3
terra nullius 91
Thacker, Eugene 21

theology of becoming 88, 90, 99
theophanic 30
Tournier, Michel 44
tradition (Christian) 83–100

unconscious/consciousness 26, 82, 102, 106
univocity 17–23, 31, 35, 49, 62, 64, 95, 102

Van Bladel, Louis 133
virtual 14–15, 23, 27–8, 36, 45, 62, 64, 68, 72, 74–80, 82, 84, 91–4
vita activa 68, 119
vita contemplative 68, 119

Westhelle, Vitor 90
Whitehead, Alfred North 76–80, 93, 96
Williams, James 15, 76–7

Žižek, Slavoj 42

www.ingramcontent.com/pod-product-compliance
Lightning Source LLC
Chambersburg PA
CBHW052049300426
44117CB00012B/2051